ALL IN

ALL IN

Texas Hold'em as Played on Late-Night TV

Anthony Holden

Weidenfeld & Nicolson
LONDON

First published in Great Britain in 2005
by Weidenfeld & Nicolson

1 3 5 7 9 10 8 6 4 2

A CIP catalogue record for this book
is available from the British Library.

ISBN-13 9 780297 852551
ISBN-10 0 297 852558

Printed and bound in Italy

Weidenfeld & Nicolson

The Orion Publishing Group Ltd
Orion House
5 Upper Saint Martin's Lane
London, WC2H 9EA

The tables in Chapter 2 and 4 draw gratefully on charts in *Poker Nation*
by Andy Bellin (2003), *The Pocket Idiot's Guide to Texas Hold'em* by
Randy Burgess and Carl Baldassarre (2004) and such websites as
http://www.learn-texas-holdem.com/.

The Orion Publishing Group's policy is to use papers that are natural,
renewable and recyclable products and made from wood grown in
sustainable forests. The logging and manufacturing processes are expected
to conform to the environmental regulations of the country of origin.

www.orionbooks.co.uk

My thanks to Cindy Blake for her thoughts re women players. Joe Holden also made many valuable contributions to this book, but spent far too much time playing online poker to be able to concentrate effectively on the job in hand. He is living proof that playing poker is far more fun than writing or indeed reading about it.

Contents

1

All to Play for

On 14 July 2005, at Binion's Casino in downtown Las Vegas, an Australian chiropractor named Joseph Hachem won $7.5 million by beating 5,618 other poker players to the title of No-Limit Hold'em World Champion. The eight other contenders at the tournament's final table all became dollar millionaires. Whoever said that gambling doesn't pay?

Thirty-five years ago, when the legendary Benny Binion hosted the first World Series of Poker (WSOP) at his Horseshoe Casino, the field of runners amounted to a mere six, the prize purse a paltry $30,000. Today, the WSOP No-Limit Hold'em Championship is, in terms of participants and prizes, the world's largest single competitive sporting event – and still growing, at an annual rate of over 200 per cent consecutively for the last three years. The prize money – $52,818,600 (around £30 million) for the Main Event alone – dwarfs that of any other sporting championship.

However talented you may be at any particular sport, let's face it: the chances of your contesting its world championship are slim to none. To play in the WSOP Main Event, however, all you need is the $10,000 entry fee and a plane ticket to Vegas – these days, not even that. The championships of 2003 and 2004 were both won by players who had earned their seats for pocket change via smaller tournaments online.

At no other sport is the opportunity to compete (and win) against the greatest players in the world so readily available – at such small prices, and for such large rewards. Hachem put up his $10,000 entry fee himself, but his prize money for a week's work was many times that of Tiger Woods for winning the Open golf tournament the same weekend or Roger Federer's for conquering Wimbledon earlier that month.

In terms of active participants, poker is beyond question the world's favourite game. Seventy-five million people (1.25 per cent of the global population) are said to play regularly – four million of them in Britain, a high proportion of them women. The game's universal appeal, transcending sport's traditional gender barriers, lies in its uniquely democratic spirit. You can sit down to play poker anywhere in the world, with a table of millionaires and hoboes, and the game's eternal verities immediately render everyone equal.

Poker is played against other people, not a bookmaker or casino, so can truly be said to be the only form of gambling where, if you know what you're doing, you are wagering favourable odds. Lady Luck may (and will) turn against you from time to time; but an expert, if he or she plays accurately and carefully, will win more often than lose. Connoisseurs of the game suggest that poker comes down to 80 per cent skill, 20 per cent luck.

In poker, most significantly of all, you don't need the best cards to win. Bet the right amount at the right time, and you can push your opponents out of the pot without even showing your cards. In no other game is licensed larceny such a bonus. Thanks to its unique element of bluff, which sets it apart from all other card games and sporting activities, poker is the only game where you can hold the worst hand but still win all the dough.

In poker, more often than not, skill triumphs over luck – unlike other forms of gambling, from the National Lottery to the gee-gees, or other casino games such as craps, roulette and blackjack, in all of which the odds are heavily stacked against you. That's not to say luck doesn't play a role in poker – of course it does; but the best players make their own.

With guile, perception, courage, patience and grit – between them, a definition of what the top players call 'heart' – you too can bend the odds in your favour and learn to beat the game, maybe even win a fortune at the turn of a card or click of a mouse.

After its introduction to the USA back in the 1820s by French sailors landing in Louisiana, poker became the preserve of a select few in the movies, usually westerns, and dubious characters in smoke-filled rooms who were probably out to cheat you – or would draw a gun if you won their money.

With the advent of legal gaming in Nevada in the 1930s, the game gradually became more honest. You could still get bilked in a back room in Chicago; but playing in casinos, or your own home game, was usually straight – and a welcome way of escaping your everyday woes. Today, in a

Doyle Brunson

The 'granddaddy' of the modern game, Brunson has lived the most significant life in poker. Born in Longworth, Texas, in 1933, he was a talented track athlete and basketball player whose hopes of joining the NBA were abruptly shattered along with his knee in an accident in a gypsum factory, where he was working pre-season. To earn a livelihood he turned to gambling, famously travelling through Texas with Brian 'Sailor' Roberts and 'Amarillo Slim' Preston playing high-stakes poker in the fifties and sixties, outrunning the law and the outlaws who preyed on illegal big-money back-room action. All three of the so-called 'Texas Rounders' would win the WSOP No-Limit Main Event within its inaugural decade, but only Brunson would win it twice, consecutively in 1976 and 1977. On both occasions, his winning hole cards in the final championship hand were 10-2, now nicknamed the 'Doyle Brunson'. The following year, he published the secrets of his success in the greatest manual ever written – *Super System* – which invited contributions from world-class players and revolutionised societal perceptions of poker from a game of luck to a game of skilful subtlety. He has recently published a follow-up, *Super System 2*, updated for the modern game, while in between volumes he upped his collection of WSOP bracelets to a record ten (tied with Johnny Chan after the 2005 WSOP). Play with Doyle on his website Doylesroom and you'll be gambling with a true legend, whose life encapsulates the evolution of the game from its nefarious Wild West roots to its global presence today.

regulated casino, you're not going to get cheated; online, it's unlikely, except in extreme circumstances.

Even a decade ago, few could have foreseen the recent and phenomenal growth of the game, which has seen the World Series of Poker expand from a convention of a small number of hardened pros into the truly international bonanza it is today. Is it really the measure of the world's best poker player? Probably not. Over a week of gruelling tournament play, twelve to fourteen hours a day, luck plays as significant a part as skill. But you can't win it without knowing what you are doing; and the prize money means that everyone who's anyone in the poker world – and more, many more – all want to take a shot at the title. And the golden bracelet that goes with it.

In the 1980s, as the World Series grew, a tournament circuit developed, breeding some two hundred professionals, mostly in the western United States, who earned a handsome living from the game. Now, suddenly, there are thousands of pros – and many more amateurs also seeking and earning handsome money, sometimes fortunes.

Over the last few years, thanks to the Internet, the poker universe has been expanding at a thousand pots a second. Around $100 million is now wagered online every day. Websites like Partypoker reportedly earn £500 a minute. The recent flotation of its parent company, Partygaming, on the London stock exchange was the UK's biggest IPO in five years. Valued at over £5.5 million, more than British Airways and ICI combined, the company catapulted straight into the FTSE 100 in the autumn of 2005. With Internet poker expanding at a rate of 16 per cent a month, the popularity of online gaming, and poker in particular, is credited with a major role in rejuvenating the 'new' economy.

Since the game's reincarnation online, television coverage has helped poker to explode. Frenzied competition between websites offers famous players lucrative sponsorship deals – and the pros can't believe their luck. Former champs from Doyle Brunson to Phil Hellmuth Jr have turned themselves into techno cottage industries, producing 'how to' guides, hosting tournaments online, running pricey Vegas boot camps for hungry students of the game, even lecturing at the venerable Oxford Union.

Where once it was a seedy, disreputable pursuit, poker is now not just respectable but fashionable, even chic, with many showbiz names on both sides of the Atlantic showing off their supposed skills on television, many alongside you in card rooms. A recent British celebrity tournament at the Palm Beach Casino in London featured golfer Sam Torrance, footballer Teddy Sheringham, actor Michael Greco and snooker players Jimmy White, Mark Williams and Ken Doherty.

Numerous Hollywood players range from veteran Oscar-nominated actor James Woods to Tobey 'Spider-man' Mcguire, both of whom played in the 2005 WSOP – as did pro golfer Rocco Mediate. Actress Jennifer Tilly won the women's title, with Mimi Rogers also performing well in various events. Ben Affleck has won a major tournament; he and his pal Matt Damon head the growing list of the Hollywood community turning to poker as relaxation, even an alternative lifestyle. Other members of the Hollywood poker set include Leonardo DiCaprio, Jack Black, Heather Graham, David Schwimmer and Martin Sheen.

At the time of writing, there is at least one major Hollywood poker movie set for release late in 2005 and a slew of others at all stages of pre-production. Tune in to the UK's Challenge TV or several other cable and terrestrial channels any night of the week and you'll find an array of poker shows, from coverage of the WSOP via the globe-trotting *World Poker Tour* to homegrown fare like Partypoker's gangsteresque East End *Poker Den* or celebrity *Late Night Poker*.

After launching on Channel 4 in 1998, *Late Night Poker* astonished its Cardiff-based production company by attracting millions of viewers in the wee small hours of Saturday nights to Sunday mornings. The secret was the glass panel revealing the players' cards to below-table cameras, enabling the TV audience to join in the cut and thrust of the game.

The third series in 2000 was launched with a celebrity special, which has since spawned countless imitators. The seven players who started with £1,000 each were actor and writer Stephen Fry, novelist Martin Amis, playwright Patrick Marber, TV comic Ricky Gervais, journalist Victoria Coren and authors (of books about, among many other things, poker) Al Alvarez and, yes, Anthony Holden.

Alvarez and I were the final men standing, with a pair of 6s proving enough for your correspondent finally to beat his old pal to the £7,000 up for grabs. Like I always say: if you're going to win a tournament, try to do it on TV.

It was Alvarez who wrote the first great literary treatise on poker and its World Series, a series of articles for the *New Yorker* magazine which became a book entitled *The Biggest Game in Town*, published in 1983. Seminal poker texts, from Herbert O. Yardley's classic *The Education of a Poker Player* to the book that improved more people's games than any other, two-time World Champ Doyle ('Texas Dolly') Brunson's *Super System*, heralded today's voluminous library of memoirs, biographies of great players and manuals on just about every variation and sub-detail of the game.

My own book *Big Deal*, an account of the year I attempted to earn my living as a professional player back in the late 1980s, has led to numerous encounters with total strangers who've credited me with inspiring them to take up the game, move to Vegas, even give up their jobs and turn professional – many of whom, I admit through gritted teeth, have made out far better than me. Now I'm at work on a sequel, entitled (of course) *Bigger Deal*.

Maybe you've read one or more of those books. More likely, you've caught the poker bug from the game's fast-growing TV coverage – revolutionised in 2003 by the arrival of the more streamlined 'pocket-cam', which enables the viewer to see the cards each player is holding.

So here comes the first important lesson this book has to offer: poker is not much like it looks on television. A one- or two-hour TV edit of a much longer contest is clearly going to zero in on the big hands – the largest pots, the moment the celebrities got knocked out, those hands where the centre of chip gravity shifted decisively.

The final table (nine players) of the 2005 World Series, for instance, wound up running for a record fourteen hours before Joe Hachem finally won through. When you see that long, hard-fought, gruelling marathon on TV, it will have been edited down to two hours.

Poker is a game of infinite, constantly changing moods

and rhythms. It can, in other words – often should – be boring. But there are worse ways to be bored, and countless things you can do while you are. Poker requires, as much as aggression or a poker face, infinite patience. Where bridge is a card game in which you can bet, poker is a game of wagering played with cards. It is a game less of luck or chance than of situations, for which you simply have to wait. The right one may take its time coming, but it will come. This book will try to help you recognise that moment, and be ready for it.

While you're waiting, there's plenty of fun to be had: joshing with the other players, watching and noting their styles of play, calculating your next move. It may all seem a bit intimidating at first, but this book will try to help you master the game before tackling it, or refine your game if you have already begun, so you can sit down to play with confidence – whether in a home game, casino or online, cash games or tournaments.

Poker is also a game with a language all its own. I will usually explain terms as I go along, but there's a glossary at the back to consult whenever you're confused.

All In is a guide to the most widely played variant of poker, Texas Hold'em: how to play it and how to win – when to hold'em, when to fold'em, as the Kenny Rogers song runs – whether you're looking to nickel-and-dime your friends, cash in at local casinos, mint it online, or even capture the Vegas crown.

It takes a moment to learn, as the saying goes, but a lifetime to master. Well, this is our moment. With fortunes out there for the taking, you gotta ask yourself: why aren't you in the game? With the help of this book, you soon will be.

2

How to Play

In poker, as in life, there is a hierarchy. This you must know by rote. A poker hand is always made up of the best five cards available to you. So the first thing to do is read, mark, learn and inwardly digest that hierarchy, from worst to best:

The Ranking of Hands

50%

High-card
no cards of the same denomination, no five of any one suit, the winning hand defined by the highest card(s),

is beaten by

43%

one pair
two cards of the same denomination – the higher the
pair, the better,

is beaten by

1:21
48%

two pairs
two x two cards of the same denomination, the highest upper pair deciding between such hands,

is beaten by

1:47
2%

three of a kind
three cards of the same denomination, or 'trips' – the
higher, the better,

is beaten by

1:255
0.4%

a straight

five consecutive cards of different suits, which can begin or end at the ace (A-2-3-4-5 or 10-J-Q-K-A) but cannot run through the ace (K-A-2-3-4), the higher the sequence, the better,

is beaten by

a flush

1:509
0.2%

five cards of the same suit, the highest card(s) deciding,

is beaten by

a full house

1:694
0.1%

three of a kind + a pair, the trips deciding the winner,

is beaten by

four of a kind

four cards of the same denomination – the higher, the better,

1:4165

is beaten by

Player Profile:

Daniel Negreanu

The most recognisable of the new generation of poker pros, Canadian-born Negreanu exploded onto the WSOP scene in 1998, winning the first ever event he played in: the $2,000 Pot-Limit Hold'em tournament. He was twenty-three years old. Originally from Toronto, he started playing at fifteen, turned pro at nineteen and has won three WSOP bracelets since moving to Vegas to play full-time. His famously close relationship with his mother led to his buying her a house in Vegas so he might benefit from her home-cooked food and packed meals on tournament days. In 2004, he was named Player of the Year by *Card Player* magazine (to which he has contributed over 100 articles), the US cable network ESPN and the World Poker Tour, after wining the $2,000 WSOP Limit Hold'em event, the $10,000 No-Limit Hold'em Championship at the Las Vegas Plaza and two WPT events: the $10,000 No-Limit Hold'em Borgata Open and the $15,000 No-Limit Hold'em Five-Diamond World Poker Classic. Credited with an uncanny ability to read his opponents, Negreanu's game is based around a cultivated aura of unpredictability. He has a reputation for being able to turn even the most unlikely hole cards into solid gold. His poker blog can be found at fullcontactpoker.com.

a straight flush
five consecutive cards of the same suit, ranked according to the highest top card,

is beaten by

a royal flush
top five consecutive cards of the same suit.

A straight flush is a rare event indeed, a royal flush a
once-in-a-lifetime hand. If you ever come up against one
in a Hold'em game, you'll lose as much money as the fortunate player holding it can sucker out of you. If you ever
hold such a hand yourself at Hold'em, silently give thanks
to the poker gods and pray that your opponent(s) call
your well-judged bet on the river. This is the ultimate
example of what they call a 'monster hand'.

Not sure what the 'river' is yet? Don't worry. You soon
will be. Betting patterns, too, can wait till the next
chapter. For now, concentrate on the ranking of hands, on
making your knowledge of that hierarchy second nature.
These are the only lines you have to learn by heart to be
able to perform poker. The rest consists of subtleties that
you'll go on learning for ever. Poker is a game where every
master of the game is still also its student. In poker, yes,

there is a hierarchy. But it can, as in life, be beaten.

Soon the ranking of hands will become subliminal. For now, just ask yourself which player is winning the following hand. In Hold'em, each player is first dealt two face-down 'hole cards', known only to himself. When the initial bet – 'the blind' – has been called (see p. 43), a card from the deck is 'burned' by the dealer (or discarded face down, to prevent cheating), and a 'flop' is then dealt.

The Flop

'The flop' is the name for the first three communal cards, dealt face up in the middle of the table. Players use their two concealed hole cards together with the three cards available to all players to make a five-card hand – with two more still to come, as we will see. For now, remember: no matter what variation of poker you're playing, no matter how many cards are available to you, your final hand will always be the best five cards on offer. Right? So who's winning here?

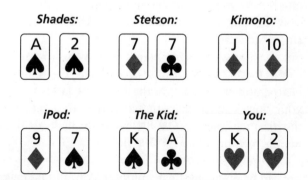

With A-K, or 'big slick' (see box, p. 38), The Kid is bound
to play the hand even if he's worried that another player
might have a pair – as does Stetson. But sevens are only a
medium-sized pair. Either one of these two may raise, but
Shades and Kimono both have decent, suited hands – as
do you, although yours is the weakest pre-flop. If there's
any action at all, which seems highly likely, iPod should
fold. Now here comes the flop.

The flop:

This a great flop for you. Here's why:
- Shades has a pair of aces, but he's being beaten by
- Stetson, who now has a 'set', or three of a kind, with
  'trip' sevens.
- Kimono has four cards to an 'inside' straight (7-9-10-
  J). She needs an 8 to complete it.
- iPod (a 'loose' player who has wrongly stayed in the
  hand) has two pairs, sevens and nines.
- The Kid has a pair of aces with a king 'kicker', or
  strong side-card;
- but you are winning the hand, with a flush in hearts
  (A♥-K♥-9♥-7♥-2♥). Since you have the king of
  hearts, and the ace is 'on the board', you also know
  your flush cannot be bettered. Any player with two
  hearts in the hole (say Q♥-8♥) would be likely to lose a
  bundle to your higher A♥-K♥ flush.

There can be no higher flush out there. You should make

a strong bet (or raise) at this point because (for now) you are holding 'the nuts', the best hand. But it might swiftly get worse, as we shall see in a minute, after we've taken a look at:

The Nuts

What each player seeks is the nuts, the Holy Grail of hands, the best cards available. Consider the following three-card flops and try to work out which hole cards would be strongest? What hand would give you the nuts?

Flop 1:

You'll notice that no two 'pocket' cards can connect a sequence of five consecutively to make a straight. Nor is a flush available, as there are no three cards of any one suit. So the best cards to be holding in your hand would be K-K, since this would give you top three of a kind, or trips. Other strong hands (in descending order) would be J-J, 2-2, K-J, K-2 or J-2. But having the second-best hand gets you nowhere in poker. It's worse than holding 'rags'. If it comes to a showdown, your hand must beat all others at the table to win.

Flop 2:

On this flop, you'll see that 8-9 in your hand would give you a low straight (8-9-10-J-Q), which would of course be beaten by 9-K (or a higher straight, 9-10-J-Q-K) or, best of all, A-K (the top straight, 10-J-Q-K-A). So A-K, or big slick, would be the nuts here, likely to win good money off a lower straight.

Flop 3:

The first thing to notice is that, thanks to the flop, every player is already holding a pair of queens. A single ace in the hole would give you a pair of aces and queens. But a single Q (one of only two remaining in the deck) would be better, giving you three of a kind, or trip queens.

A pair of aces (A♥-A♦) in the hole (a.k.a. 'aces wired') would give you a powerful 'boat', or full house, trip aces + paired queens (A-A-A-Q-Q). But even that would be beaten by a player holding pocket queens (a pair of queens in the hole). The odds against it are high (see table, p. 35), leaving the 'boat' in danger of losing a lot of money, but pocket queens would give their fortunate possessor an unbeatable (at this stage) four of a kind, or 'quad' queens (Q♥-Q♦-Q♠-Q♣) – the nuts. This hand could go wrong over the next two communal cards, but it is highly unlikely.

Hold'em: a Card-by-card Breakdown

You've seen how hole cards combine with the cards dealt on the flop to make a poker hand; but in Hold'em each player makes the best five-card hand out of their two hole cards and not just three, but five communal cards. After the first three are dealt, there follows a fourth (known as 'fourth street', or 'the turn') and then final communal card (known as 'fifth street', or 'the river'). So each player has a total of seven cards available to them, out of which the best five represent their hand.

Let's pick up on our earlier example, as the fourth communal card is added to the flop in the centre of the table. You're winning for now. But will you win the hand?

The turn brings an 8♠.

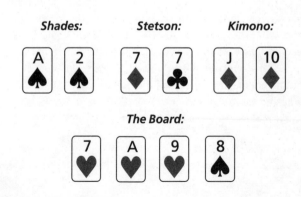

Shades: *Stetson:*   *Kimono:*

A♠ 2♠   7♦ 7♣   J♦ 10♦

The Board:

7♥ A♥ 9♥ 8♠

Player Profile:

Phil Ivey

A quiet player, and a reportedly shy man, Ivey is known for his total concentration and ruthless aggression at the poker table, which has won him a reputation as the most talented and fearsome of young pros. Oft-called 'the Tiger Woods of poker', Ivey disowns the nickname, saying: 'Tiger's the best at his game. I'm not there yet.' After growing up in New Jersey, Ivey won his first WSOP gold bracelet in 2000 playing Pot Limit Omaha at the age of twenty-three. In 2002, he won three more, tying Phil Hellmuth and Ted Forrest's record for most wins in a single year, and in 2005 he won a fifth in the $5,000 Pot Lmit Omaha event. In 2003, he placed tenth in the Main Event (despite an incredibly bad beat by Chris Money-maker – see pp. 112–13), finished second in the World Poker Open and third in the inaugural World Poker Tour championship. 'Money is nice,' he says. 'That's very important. That's the reward. But you've got to play because you love the game. That's the difference between a good player and a great player. Once you start playing for the love of the game, what the game has to offer, its different challenges, then you'll be able to take your game to the next level.' Ivey is one of the quorum of established greats sponsored to play at fulltiltpoker.com in perhaps the game's most far-reaching marketing campaign yet. Formerly resident in Atlantic City, he now makes his home in Los Angeles.

iPod: *The Kid:*   *You:*

This 8♠ is a very useful card for you. Kimono has made her 'gutshot' straight, but is losing to your flush. So you're still ahead. But then fifth street, or the river, brings a 9♣.

Shades: *Stetson:*   *Kimono:*

The Board:

iPod: *The Kid:*   *You:*

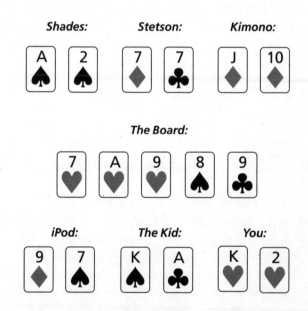

This last card is disastrous for you – because two players now have full houses, which beat your flush. Stetson has a low full house (7-7-7-9-9), sevens full of nines. But iPod (who should never have called the first bet) will win the hand with nines full of sevens (9-9-9-7-7). And what would the nuts be? Why, paired nines in the hole (giving you four of a kind), which hasn't happened here, and rarely will. If this game were televised, a viewer would have known that two players held aces, which diminishes the odds on the flop against a full house aces full of nines (A-A-A-9-9) emerging. However, no single player in the hand could have known this, so that full house would have remained a remote but dangerous possibility after the flop.

Note that whenever a pair has fallen on the board (i.e. when the board itself is paired), a full house (and a less likely four of a kind) becomes a possible hand. And always remember that the board can win. If no one still in the hand can improve on the five cards in the middle, the pot is split between those still playing at the end (or 'showdown').

Hold'em: Another Sample Hand

Now let's look at another example to see how the nuts can change as first three (the flop), then four (the turn), then five (the river) communal cards make up the board.

After the initial deal, each player is holding:

Shades: *Stetson:*   *Kimono:*

K♥ K♦   6♦ 7♣   Q♥ 9♥

iPod: *The Kid:*   *You:*

The flop comes:

So, at this point, Shades has boss trips (K-K-K), while iPod has a potentially expensive trip fours. Kimono has four cards to a straight (9-10-Q-K), in need of a jack to fill it. You also have four cards to a straight (10-J-Q-K). The Kid has ace-high and four cards to a spade flush. Stetson is holding rags (i.e. nothing worth having), though he could make an unlikely straight by the final river card (6-7-8-9-10).

Ostensibly you have a decent 'draw'. You are drawing to an 'open-ended' straight, i.e. a card on either side of the four you already have in sequence – either an ace or a 9 – would fill up your straight. Kimono (again) has a lesser 'inside straight', or gutshot draw. Only a jack would fill her straight. Regardless, Shades is in powerful position and betting at you, as fourth street (the turn) brings a J♣. Now the board reads:

Who's winning now? This is a lively hand. Lucky old Kimono has filled her straight (9-10-J-Q-K) and is ahead. You now have paired jacks to go with your inside straight draw. The Kid now has four cards to a flush and a straight. iPod and Shades both have trips, and are looking for the board to pair – to make a full house or four of a kind. Stetson has lost the hand; he is, as they say, 'drawing dead'. No card that could fall on the river would give him a winning hand. He's lost even before fifth street brings a 9♠:

You've now made your straight, the same straight as Kimono. Maybe you'll both end up splitting the pot with 9-10-J-Q-K? Then again, maybe not. Just for the record, here are each player's final hands:

Shades:

Trip kings

Stetson:

King-high

Kimono:

Straight

iPod:

Trip fours

The Kid:

Flush – WINNER!

You

Straight

The Kid has won the hand with an unbeatable 'nut flush' or ace-high flush in spades. He wins all the money – and you, if you care to call his bet, could wind up losing a fortune.

Player Profile:

Annie Duke

Considered the best all-round female player, Duke was introduced to poker by her two-time WSOP bracelet-winning brother Howard ('The Professor') Lederer (see p. 34). When she played in her first World Series in 1995, she placed in three events and knocked Lederer out of the Main Event. She has since become the top female WSOP money winner in history, winning $2 million in the auspicious inaugural WSOP invitational Tournament of Champions last year and, after conquering the Bellagio's $2,500 Limit Hold'em tournament, her first gold bracelet in the 2005 $2,000 Hi/Lo Omaha event. Famously, she finished tenth in the 2000 WSOP Main Event while eight months pregnant. Alongside Phil Hellmuth Jr, Dave 'Devilfish' Ulliott, Lederer and former WSOP tournament director Jack McClelland, Duke is one of 'Team UB', the auspicious array of pros sponsored to play at ultimatebet.com. Her former poker tutee, actor Ben Affleck, has also been known to play on the site. Duke's poker journal can be found at annieduke.com.

The Nuts Revisited: from Flop to River

Hold'em, you will have noticed, is a game where any hand may be winning one minute, then losing the next. Study another sample, to see how the lead in any one hand can change dramatically:

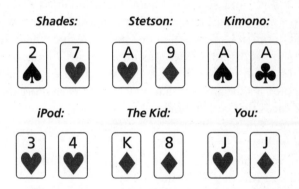

Before the flop's been dealt, your hole cards should give you a clue as to whether you may be able to make a strong hand. Shades has 2-7 off-suit, theoretically the worst hole cards in Hold'em because it doesn't even hook up for the lowest possible straight. Kimono is currently winning with the best possible pre-flop hand, pocket aces. iPod has low 'suited-connectors', two cards that could well make a flush or a straight. Stetson has an ace, with an unsuited, middling kicker. The Kid has an unexciting, if suited, king, while you have a strong hand with paired jacks. Notice how, if hole cards are suited (as with iPod's and The Kid's), they have a far better chance of making a flush. The flop brings:

Take a moment to consider this flop. Whose hand would you like to be holding if you saw these three cards on the board? Would you care to be iPod, with four cards to both flush and straight draws? Or Kimono, with boss trips? At this stage of the hand, it's impossible to tell who will ultimately win it – but, since she has the nuts, Kimono is definitely the odds-on favourite. In any hand of Hold'em, as you'll see when we come to the next chapter, it's the amount that players bet – even more than the cards they are holding – that will decide the ultimate winner. For now, though of course you don't know it, you're losing, since your jacks are bettered by Kimono's trip aces, Stetson's pair of aces and The Kid's paired kings, as fourth street brings a 2♦:

Suddenly, The Kid is excited by the prospect of his diamond flush-draw. He has the king of diamonds and the ace is already on the board, so he knows no other flush will beat him if the river brings a diamond. iPod is still hanging in with four cards to a straight and four to a flush. Shades (who should have folded his 7-2 before the flop) now has low trips. Stetson, The Kid and you all have two pairs. But you're all going down to Kimono, who has aces full of deuces, until fifth street falls:

Yes, everything has changed again. No flush is possible, since the board is showing no three cards of the same suit. No straight is possible. Everyone's got trip deuces and anyone with a pair has a full house. You have twos (or 'deuces') full of jacks, beaten by The Kid's twos full of kings, beaten by Stetson's twos full of aces – and all these have been busted by Kimono's aces full of deuces. But this river card was a disaster for her, because it turned Shades' trip deuces into quad deuces. He's won the hand – but would he have ever been in it? Imagine the embarrassment of turning over 7-2 to claim all that dough …

Shades:

Four of a kind – WINNER!

Stetson:

Full house

Kimono:

Full house

iPod:

Three of a kind (playing the board)

The Kid:

Full house

You:

Full house

Before I explain why that hand would never really happen – because Shades would not even have called the opening blind, let alone Kimono's pre-flop raise – here are some sample hands to help you master the reading of the cards, and some tables giving statistical guides to the odds against being dealt certain hands, and their improving on the flop.

As with the ranking of hands, you should study these until they are engraved on your subconscious.

Sample Hold'em: Best Hands

Example 1:
The Board:

Hole Cards
1. Q♠-9♠ (Straight flush)
2. 9♠-7♠ (Straight flush)
3. A♠-A♣ (Four of a kind)
4. A-J (Full house)
5. A-10 (Full house)

Example 2:
The Board:

Hole Cards
1. 2♦-2♣ (Four of a kind)
2. K-K (Full house)
3. Q-Q (Full house)
4. 10-10 (Full house)
5. A-J (Top straight)

Example 3:
The Board:

Hole Cards
1. 10-8   (Top straight)
2. 8-5   (Straight)
3. 5-3   (Low straight)
4. Q-Q   (Three of a kind)
5. 9-9   (Three of a kind)

Example 4:
The Board:

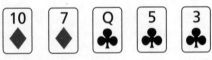

Hole Cards
1. A♣-x♣ (Nut flush)
2. K♣-x♣ (Flush)
3. J♣-x♣ (Flush)
4. 10♣-x♣ (Flush)
5. 9♣-x♣ (Flush)

Recognised Odds Against Being Dealt Strong to Medium Hole Cards

Pocket Pairs:*

A-A	220–1
K-K	110–1
Q-Q	72–1
J-J	72–1
10-10	46–1
9-9	46–1
8-8	46–1
7-7	46–1
6-6	46–1
5-5	46–1
4-4	46–1
3-3	46–1
2-2	46–1

Suited Connectors:

A-K	330–1
K-Q	330–1
Q-J	330–1
J-10	46–1
10-9	46–1
9-8	46–1
8-7	46–1
6-5	46–1
5-4	46–1

* The odds against being dealt *any* pair are 16–1, but obviously this varies according to the seniority of any *particular* pair.

Howard Lederer

Lederer deferred college to move to New York to follow his passion for chess and, after discovering a poker game in the back room of his favourite chess club, got hooked on that too. Alongside Dan Harrington and Erik Seidel, Lederer played a major role in establishing No-Limit Hold'em as the game of choice at New York's legendary Mayfair Club in the mid-eighties. After moving to Las Vegas in 1993, he and his sister, Annie Duke (see p. 26), made history after being the first siblings to make the same final table the following year. Nicknamed 'The Professor' on account of his thoughtful, serious demeanour, Lederer won WSOP titles in $5,000 Hi/Lo Omaha in 2000 and $5,000 seven-card draw the following year. He hosts a regular table at fulltiltpoker.com and is the creator of an instructional video *Secrets of No-Limit Hold'em*. A selection of his incisive articles on the game can be found at howardlederer.com.

Other Strong Starting Hands:

A-K off-suit	110–1
A-Q suited	165–1
A-Q off-suit	55–1
A-J suited	165–1
A-J off-suit	55–1
K-Q off-suit	110–1
A-10 or less, suited	36–1
A-10 or less, off-suit	11–1
A-anything	5.5–1
ANY pair	16–1
ANY two cards suited	3.25–1
ANY suited connectors	47–1
ANY off-suit connectors	15–1
ANY hand with a pair, or an ace	4–1

Odds Against Flopping:

Quads	with a pocket pair	407–1
Flush	with suited cards	118–1
Straight	with 9-5 off-suit	305–1
	with 8-5 off-suit	152–1
	with 7-5 off-suit	101–1
	with 6-5 off-suit	76–1
Three of a kind	with a pocket pair	8.3–1
One pair	with ace + K/Q/J/10	2.5–1
Flush draw	with suited ace + kicker	8.1–1
Straight draw	with off-suit connectors	7.5–1
Straight/flush draw	with suited connectors	2.5–1

Poker Wisdom

Once you've mastered these fundamental truths, commit to memory two immortal poker sayings:

'Never play with mugs' – i.e. players who don't know what they're doing, because they're likely to chuck their money in on anything, and may well prove lucky enough to beat your strong, well-played hand. It's more fun, believe it or not, playing with skilled players – just as long as they are less skilled than you.

But, before you get too cocky, be sure to remember: 'If you can't spot the sucker in your first half-hour at the table … it's you!'

3

How to Win

The good news, as I've always maintained, is that in every deck of fifty-two cards there are 2,598,960 possible five-card poker hands. The bad news is that you are going to be dealt only one of them. The following table gives an approximate guide to the relative chances of being dealt a particular hand in any variant of five-card poker, including Hold'em (at, of course, the flop, after which they vary slightly):

Quantity in Deck		Odds Against
4	Royal flush	649,739–1
40	Straight flush	64,973–1
624	Four of a kind	4,164–1
3,744	Full house	693–1
5,108	Flush	508–1
10,200	Straight	254–1
54,912	Three of a kind	46–1
123,552	Two pairs	20–1
1,098,240	One pair	1.25–1
1,302,540	No pair	EVENS

Nicknames of Pocket Hands

A-A	American Airlines
A-K	Big Slick
A-Q	Big Chick
A-J	Ajax, or Jackass
A-10	Johnny Moss
A-8	Dead Man's Hand
K-K	Cowboys
K-Q	Royal Wedding
K-J	Kojak
K-9	Canine
Q-Q	Siegfried and Roy
Q-J	Maverick
Q♠-J♦	Pinochle
Q-9	Quinine
J-5	Motown
J-4	Flat Tyre
10-4	Broderick Crawford
10-2	Doyle Brunson
9-9	German Virgins
9-5	Dolly Parton
8-8	Snowmen
7-7	Sunset Strip
6-6	Route 66
5-10	Woolworth
4-5	Jesse James
4-4-4	Grand Jury
3-8	Raquel Welch
3-3	Crabs
2-9	Twiggy
2-2	Ducks

If there were no betting in poker, the hands would just fall randomly and pointlessly, all players winning some of the time. It would be a game of pure chance. But poker is played for money, often euphemised as 'the method of keeping score'. You can play with real cash in your home game; but it's far more convenient, and better psychology, to play with chips – which can also lend some distance between the amounts of money involved and the role they might play in your everyday lives. This can be A Good Thing, in that it helps you to make better poker judgements, regardless of the amounts of money involved; or A Bad Thing, if you are constantly equating your wagers with your rent. As some wiseacre, reputedly the legendary Chicago gangster-gambler Big Julie, once said: 'The guy who invented cards was clever, but the guy who invented chips was a genius.'

In any Hold'em deal, any starting hand could theoretically evolve into the winning one. The possibilities aroused by the arrival of every new card are what give the game its unique thrill. But only by betting will you find out who actually wins – which takes the attention away from the mere cards to the much more important study of betting patterns.

In any one hand of poker, you have a maximum of five options available to you at any one time. You can:

1. Check: bet zero, possible only after the pre-flop round of betting, if no bet has yet been made. You can indicate a check either by saying the word, or rapping your knuckles or fingertips on the table.
2. Bet: wager a nominal number of chips.
3. Call: match an existing bet.

4. Raise: increase an existing bet and so the pressure on your opponents.
5. Fold: 'muck' your cards and surrender the hand.

Learning when and how much to bet – how to steal the chips already in the pot, to stop other players filling their 'pulling' hands (four-card flushes or straights), and to sucker the maximum number of chips out of your opponent when you hold an unbeatable hand – this is the essence of playing good poker.

There are five things you should keep an eagle-eye on throughout every hand:

1. How many players are in the pot?
2. Who, if anyone, has raised?
3. How much have they raised?
4. How much have they got left?
5. Your position in the betting order, relative to the dealer button, or 'buck' (see p. 43).

Poker is a game of decision-making under pressure. Even more important than the cards you hold is the amount you bet. By betting the right amount at the right moment, even with weak cards, a player 'represents' a winning hand, regardless of whether they are actually holding it. And, hey, who's to know?

The game of Hold'em involves up to four rounds of betting, which break down like this:

1. After each player is dealt their hole cards, they must call an obligatory opening bet to stay in the game. Players call, raise or fold until one is left or all bets are matched.

Player Profile:

Johnny Chan

Nicknamed the 'Orient Express', Chan was born in Canton, China, but moved to Houston with his family in 1973. He dropped out of the University of Houston aged twenty-one to move to Las Vegas to become a professional gambler. While working as a fry-chef at the Fremont Hotel, next door to Binion's, he perfected his game and became the most successful player in the world on winning the WSOP No-Limit Hold'em Championship two years running in 1987 and 1988. The following year, amazingly enough, he finished second to Phil Hellmuth. Renowned for the lucky orange he has with him at all times at the table, Chan was famously credited as being the leading Hold'em player of his time in the Hollywood movie *Rounders*. In 2005 he became the first player to win a record ten WSOP bracelets (though Doyle Brunson equalled the feat the same year). Having won WSOP championships in No-Limit Hold'em (1988, 1989, 2003), Limit Hold'em (1985), Pot-Limit Hold'em (2003 and 2005), Seven Card Stud (1994), Deuce to Seven draw (1997) and Pot-Limit Omaha (2002), Chan is thought to be the best all-round player in the world. He was inducted into the Poker Hall of Fame in 2002.

2. A down card is burned; and three communal cards –
   the flop – are dealt in the centre of the table. Players
   check, bet, call, raise or fold until one is left or all bets
   are matched.

3. A down card is burned; and the fourth communal card
   – fourth street, or the turn – is dealt. Players check,
   bet, call, raise or fold until one is left or all bets are
   matched.

4. A down card is burned; and the fifth communal card –
   fifth street, or the river – completes the board. Players
   check, bet, call, raise or fold until one is left or all bets
   are matched. Once a final bet has been called, or if the
   table has been checked right round, the player who
   shows the best hand wins the pot. Only the player
   whose bet is called is obliged to show his cards. Losing
   hands may be mucked.

Sounds straightforward enough? Maybe so. Hold'em
looks like one of the simplest variants of poker, but it is
also one of the most complex.

There are good reasons why it is a source of endless
fascination to game theorists and probability statisti-
cians. As each new communal card is revealed on the
board, the values of all the pocket hands change.

Assessing the relative value of your own cards against
those you believe your opponents are holding, at each of the
above four stages, is the essence of playing the game well.

Apart, of course, from bluffing with courage and con-
viction.

Blinds

In Hold'em, the first betting cycle of the first round is begun by two compulsory bets – the 'small blind' and the 'big blind'. The small blind is always half the big blind, say 50p in a game of £1–£2 Limit Hold'em. The big blind is in effect the opening bet, so £1 in the same game.

With up to ten players at the table – it was invented, after all, to get the maximum number involved – Hold'em is played 'off the button', i.e. the small blind sits immediately to the dealer's left and the big blind to the small blind's left, so two to the dealer's. (In 'on the button', usually played when the table is down to just two players, the dealer himself is responsible for the small blind.) Financially, as the deal rotates clockwise, it works out the same for every player, because each will 'put up' the small blind and the big blind once a round. The advantage of being either of these blinds, especially the big one, is that you have the right to raise when the betting comes round the table and back to you. In the later stages of tournament play and some high-stakes cash games, the revolving blinds are supplemented by a compulsory 'ante', which every player at the table has to put forward at the deal.

In casinos and tournament play, when you have a professional dealer, the player notionally dealing the cards is indicated by a DEALER button, which passes around the table with each hand. At a full table of Hold'em players, with a professional dealer, the seat numbers go like this:

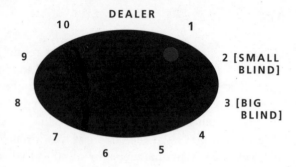

So if, as here, the DEALER button were with the player in Seat 1, Seat 2 would put up the small blind, Seat 3 the big blind and Seat 4 would be the first to act. After this hand, the dealership moves clockwise, along with the button signifying whose deal it is. Hence the phrases 'passing the buck' and 'the buck stops here', the latter famously inscribed on a plaque on Harry Truman's desk in the White House.

Position

Effective manipulation of the betting cycles is the key to winning at poker. Making efficient use of your changing position within this cycle is the best way to make this happen. As the button passes round the table, so it becomes possible to 'limp in' in late position during the first round of betting, or 'flat-call' with a lesser hand, which might come good on the flop. If you're not sure about your pre-flop 2-7 off-suit – the worst available Hold'em hand, which you should probably fold in any

Beginner's Luck

Ten tips for those still on a learning curve – in a home game or in a card room:

1. Concentrate. Even if you don't intend to play the hand, keep an eye on what's happening. Don't, for instance, fold out of turn; it annoys the other players, not least because it gives their opponents information (viz. that you're not going to play the hand).

2. Even more important, don't bet out of turn. Again, it bugs the other players – and it can cost you. Different games have different rules about these things, but you're bound to lose out – perhaps by forfeiting the right to raise if someone comes in ahead of you.

3. Keep concentrating. Just because you're not in the hand, doesn't mean you can't learn something about the other players – and the game – from the way they play it.

4. Under the same heading, always post your blind – large or small – without having to be nagged to. That, too, is very tiresome to the other players, even to the dealer (if you have one).

5. Protect your cards. Put a chip or personal talisman on your hole-cards, even if you wind up folding them. If a dealer scoops them up by mistake, it's your fault, not his. Your hand is dead – as it is if it hits the 'muck', or discarded cards, for whatever reason.

6. If you want to show your cards, wait till the hand is over – or you might get shot. If you show them to one player, maybe the guy you were up against, you must show them to all.

7. If you've bluffed someone out of a pot, showing them your cards – and thus their own mistake – is a perfectly

legitimate tactic. But do it sparingly. It gets up their noses, and they're going to come after you.

8. If you're going to raise, say so. A chip of larger denomination than the bet is deemed a call, unless you say 'Raise'. Likewise, a player with a fistful of chips in the middle, or 'across the line', cannot raise unless he pre-announces it, or indeed go back to his stack for more. A player guilty of doing this, even by mistake, is making a 'string' bet – which is illegal.

9. Don't take any notice of Kenny Rogers. Sure, you have to know when to hold 'em, know when to fold 'em. But feel free to count your money while you're sitting at the table. Knowing the size of your own stack, and indeed everyone else's, is a crucial part of playing the game well.

10. Always remember the wise words of David Mamet, and everyone else who has ever played poker. It doesn't matter who wins the most hands. It's the person who wins the most money ...

circumstances – the pot remains unraised and you can get in for cheap, will you call? What kind of player are you? Disciplined or dangerously wild? And what happens when that flop brings 2-7-A? What then?

Once the first round of betting is out of the way, the first player to act is the first player to the dealer's left who is still in the hand. If you're on the button – if, notionally, it's your deal – you will therefore have maximum advance information as to which players are representing what hands by their betting. Say someone in front of you has raised the blind before the flop, and so you've put them on ace-x ... then the flop comes A-7-7 and you're holding a 7 in the hole ... you have 'position' on your opponent, who will have to act before you for the rest of the hand.

You can wait for them to check, bet, raise or re-raise others, before deciding whether just to call (maybe they have A-A or A-7?) or (much better) to raise (maybe they've a low pocket pair or rags – i.e. they've misread you, and are making the mistake of bluffing into your strong hand with nothing).

In post-flop rounds of betting, a strong bet or well-timed raise can steal the pot when you sense weakness in your opponents' hands. And you don't even have to show them your own. This is an easier trick to pull off – be it a complete bluff or a 'semi-bluff', i.e. playing a 'pulling' hand with odds-against chances of improving – if you're in late position, if the other players have checked to you or bet 'at you' weakly.

So it follows that players are more likely to bluff or semi-bluff the closer they are to the end of the betting cycle. The practice of 'stealing the blinds' – those obligatory bets paid by the players first and second to the dealer's left – forms a key ingredient of any decent player's box of tricks, especially in late position, if no one before you has raised.

But be wary. Most players are loath to lose their blinds, especially the big one. They may well defend their blind by raising you back, as much out of stubbornness or pride as because they're holding a mean pair in the hole.

If the hand is checked round to you and you don't make a bet, large or small, other players will peg you as a mark, a 'tourist', a 'rock' – as a cautious, even gutless player who doesn't even have the good sense to *try* to steal the blinds. There may be honour at a poker table, even among thieves, but they will then bet at you more aggressively to push you out of the pot.

If your opponents are aggressive, use their aggression against them. Play patient, wait until you can limp in and flop a straight. Then let them bet at you. If your opponents play tight, use their thrift against them. Bet more than they can afford and watch out when they call. Poker is a game of paradoxes. But remember always to bully the bully.

The first lesson to learn about betting is that, if other players aren't doing it, or if they are being cautious, you should go after them with a big bet or raise, whatever cards you're holding. If you then get re-raised by a canny player lying in wait, cut your losses by folding. Varying your tactics like this, or 'mixing up' your game, is the only way to wind up winning.

Above all, don't be obvious.

Aggression

Ask a poker pro the qualities required to become a top player, and he will likely tell you patience and aggression, even ruthlessness. Patience is a major virtue; poker is a game less about cards than about situations. You have to wait for the right moment to do the right thing, though occasionally you may get lucky after doing the right thing at the wrong moment or the wrong thing at the right moment. There are few 'outs' – or escape routes, which I will explain in a minute – if you do the wrong thing at the wrong moment.

By aggression, the pro will mean …

(Stone-cold) Bluffing

Unless a player is holding the nuts – if, in theory, there's a better hand out there – then his hand is fallible and will fall to a bet of aggressive weight, most often a big bet. Aggression, aggression, aggression – with a sizable dose of perception and psychology – is invariably a winning combination.

Consider a sample hand in a £1–£2 game of No-Limit Hold'em, where players can bet as much money as they have in front of them. The cards have been dealt:

Kimono (£106)   *The Kid (£332)*   *You (£139)*

You call the blind. Kimono calls the blind and raises £5. The small blind folds and The Kid (already in for the big blind) calls. So do you. Now three players are left, with £22 in the pot, as the flop falls:

You flop 'two pair' (as poker players call two pairs) and are the first to act. Feeling sure you're ahead, you bet £10. Kimono, wary of seeing that ace on the flop, and rightly surmising you might have paired aces, just calls … because the last card she wanted to see on the flop was an

Player Profile:

Jennifer Harman

Born in Reno, Nevada, she first encountered poker kibitzing her father's home game at eight years old. She turned pro in the mid-1980s and after a disastrous early year, which led to a friend lending her $50,000, she began to make out phenomenally well, winning two WSOP gold bracelets at the 2000 Lowball Event and the 2002 $5,000 Limit Hold'em Championship. She was recently invited, along with her friend Daniel Negreanu, to contribute to Doyle Brunson's *Super System 2*. Jennifer wrote the chapter on Limit Hold'em. After undergoing a kidney transplant, she returned to the WSOP in 2005 with a vengeance, cashing in five events. She regularly plays in the $2000–$4000 Hold'em game at the Bellagio. 'In professional poker,' Harman says, 'it probably helps to be a woman. In general, most men don't think women can play.' 'The most feared female poker player in the world', according to *Sports Illustrated*, her poker journal and articles can be found at jenniferharman.com.

ace or a king, but she's still loath to give up her beautiful paired queens. Then, out of nowhere, The Kid raises £50. Why? Because he's an aggressively 'loose' player – the wild kind – who has shrewdly put you on a pair of aces and Kimono on a high pair.

He's noticed (as you should have) that the flop has made a spade flush very possible, and he's throwing out a high bet to see if either of you have any spades. With two pairs in your hand (including top pair), the Kid's raise makes you a tad indignant, but you can't shake the feeling he's already got a lock on the spade flush.

You should re-raise him; but, wrongly, you fold. As, fairly swiftly, does Kimono. The Kid – if he's feeling particularly cocky – might show you his cards to let you know how cheekily he has just stolen your money. This is called 'advertising', and is a legitimate (if not always popular) tactic to unsettle other players.

You played this hand very weakly. But here's why The Kid's move was successful, if strikingly loose play: because he bet £50, not £20 or £30. He bet more than you or Kimono were willing to gamble at this point in the hand, and so won the pot before it could go any further. 'Why did he bet so much?' you should have asked yourself. 'That's usually the sign of a bluff.' The Kid's play was doubly dangerous, first because either you or Kimono might easily have had a high spade, or pair of spades, in your hand, in which case you would have been much more likely to call; and, second, because the size of the pot didn't merit the risk of a bet that size. 'Pot odds' – the amount the pot is offering you in return for your investment – are a key element in such calculations.

When The Kid raised, the pot was £52. So he was in

effect doubling it. His pot odds – the ratio between the amount in the pot and the amount of a player's bet – were far from favourable.

Why did he get away with such an outlandish move? Maybe because The Kid has thus far projected the image of being a 'tight' player who, whenever he bets, is sure to have a hand; in other words, his previous play has given him the 'table image' of a rock, a player who plays only good hands. Or, more likely, simply because The Kid had more money than anyone else to throw around.

As in cash games, so also in tournaments, winning players have the advantage, because they have more money with which to attack the pot. A £50 call would have cost you almost half the rest of your stack, maybe committing you to investing the rest on your two pairs, while costing Kimono most of hers. So The Kid's bet, while risky, was carefully calculated. Poker can be a cruel game when you're short-stacked.

Laying Traps

At the highest level of Hold'em, you will rarely see a flop – as all the serious betting will come pre-flop, with experienced players betting and out-betting each other until one takes the pot without even revealing his cards. You should have played for a while before you get involved in such macho antics. For now, let's concentrate on the basics of post-flop betting tactics.

If the board is showing three cards of the same suit, a flush is always possible. Ditto a straight, or a straight draw, if the flop shows three cards in sequence, however high or low. If it's paired, there are full house, as well as trip and, more rarely, four of a kind possibilities. If you sense weakness in your opponent, the best way to separate them from their chips – the object of the exercise – is to bet at them.

But, remember, players with the best hands will rarely bet big immediately. If you've 7-7 in the hole and the flop comes 7-3-7, why announce your illustrious quads – an unbeatable hand if no straight flush is possible – when there are two more rounds of betting to come? You should 'slow-play' them, i.e. check, call and sucker your opponents in – taking your time in the process, giving an Oscar-winning impression that you're worried about the outcome – then raise on the river and see if they raise you back. Then you're laughing.

Let them find hands with which to bet at you. Draw their chips in, using psychology as your magnet.

Longing to wipe that cheeky grin off The Kid's face, in the very next hand you find he's betting at you again, raising £3 from the small blind. Since you're already in for the big blind, you call, as does iPod, whom you suspect may have A-x going up against The Kid's high pair.

The Kid (£362)   *You (£117)*   *iPod (£201)*

Pot: £15

The Board:

To your (very) silent satisfaction, you find you've flopped the nuts – the highest available straight. Now when The Kid bets again 'under-the-gun' – in first position after the dealer – you smile inside and, granite-faced, just call £8. Shouldn't you have raised? Not yet. You're not worried about a flush (since the flop is 'rainbow' – all different suits) and you have the nuts. iPod, with middle pair and top kicker, also calls …

And the flop brings a K♦:

Pot: £39

The Board:

Now's your moment. Not least because you can now be beaten by A-Q. The Kid, worried about a straight draw but putting you both on high pairs, bets £35, enough to win the hand. But he's miscalculated. For you, now (correctly) concerned about the chances of a diamond flush or top straight (both possibilities for iPod), have laid your trap and now it's time to bring home the bacon. There's also the chance that someone has trips (as does The Kid), and the board might pair, giving him a full house.

You raise The Kid another £35 right back at him – grinning inwardly as his face crumbles. iPod, sensing the straight's already out there and unwilling to risk £70 on the slim (33 per cent) chance she'll fill her flush or straight, folds. The Kid, though pretty sure he's losing the hand, calls your £35 in the hopes the board will pair …

Pot: £179

The Board:

Against the odds, iPod's nut flush has come up; she kicks herself for not calling, but takes consolation in the pot odds against her investment. The Kid calls and decides against raising – even though there's a flush possibility out there – when you make a 'sucker' bet of £25. He knows, with only £14 more to your name, you're bound to call any raise. You're too deep into this pot now to pull out. So your trap works and you're £121 the richer.

Though the nuts on the flop, your hand would have fallen to a top straight or a diamond flush. So was The Kid right not to try to bluff you on the river? Sure he was. Beware the short-stack, for if they are pot-committed, they're far more likely to go all in.

If you suspect you're being trapped – most commonly trap-checked – do not bet, unless a radical change comes on the board (a flush draw where previously there were only straight draws, or if the board pairs).

There was a classic example of this kind of play, immortalised in the John Dahl movie *Rounders*, when Johnny Chan suckered Eric Sidel into the pot during the head-to-head of the 1988 WSOP. Chan was dealt J♣-9♣, Sidel Q♣-7♥. Both players limped in, and the flop came Q♠-10♥-8♦. With the best possible hand, against Sidel's top pair, Chan bet a modest $40,000. Sidel, understandably, raised $50,000, and Chan just called. The turn brought an irrelevant 2♠ – and Chan just checked, in the hope that Sidel would think he was 'on the draw'. It worked. Sidel moved all in. When Chan called, and the river brought a 6♦, the reigning world champion had successfully defended his title.

Odds and Outs

Calculating your 'outs' is an important factor in deciding whether to call a big bet. The number of your outs is the number of those cards still in the deck which could win the pot for you.

If you're holding two pairs, for instance, and there's a chance your opponent may be holding a straight or a flush, you have four outs left in the deck – the other two cards of each denomination which match your own. Subtract the five cards you have seen – the two in your hand plus the three in the flop – from the fifty-two in the original deck, and that gives you four 'outs' in forty-seven cards, or slightly less than a 12–1 chance of making your boat. Set that against the pot odds you are being offered, likely to be less than that, and you have the basis on which to make your decision.

These odds naturally narrow somewhat after the turn, i.e. with only one card to come, rather than two.

In other situations, you may easily have many more outs. You're holding, for instance, A♠-8♠ and you're still in the pot when the flop brings A♥-K♠-2♠. Now you're not merely holding top pair, with a medium kicker, but four to a flush. You put your opponent on a king in the hole, paired by the flop. So now your outs include all nine spades you haven't yet seen, plus the two remaining aces, and the three remaining 8s – a total of fourteen out of forty-seven, or better than 3.5–1 that you'll beat K-2, or two pairs. That's a call or raise you might well consider making.

Now, before the next chapter, take a break – or fix yourself a stiff drink. It's time to blind you with statistics.

4

Figuring the Odds

Dazzled by all these statistics? You ain't seen nuttin' yet.

Soon I'm going to blind you with science – a sequence of tables showing the approximate odds of certain hands winning a pot, and/or improving at each stage of the deal. Only a maths genius could commit them to memory – and no, you can't keep them handy beside you at the table – but studying them will give you a better feel for the relative values of the many, many hands you're going to be seeing over the years.

First, a beginner's guide to betting, which should give you some ideas about when and why and how much to bet at any stage of a single Hold'em hand. Get a feel for this, and then study the values of the hands available, pre- and post-flop. Remember, these are only guidelines. Every player of quality has their own style, their own tricks up their sleeve – and you too must hone and polish yours to be a winner.

Player Profile:

Phil Hellmuth Jr

When he won the WSOP Main Event in 1989 at just twenty-four years of age – the youngest player ever to do so – he'd been saying he'd win it for the previous year. In fact, he'd been saying he'd win it for the previous several years. The son of a university professor, the self-styled 'John McEnroe' of poker has taken greater advantage of the global poker explosion than anyone else, becoming the game's best-known international ambassador, alongside authoring two strategy guides, creating an instructional DVD and now running Vegas boot camps in association with other top pros. He has nine WSOP gold bracelets, has cashed in forty-eight events and won over £2 million in the World Series alone. He can be found on the web at philhellmuth.com. His autobiography *Poker Brat* will soon be with us.

Betting: Some Guidelines, Card-by-card

Pre-flop

Call (just the blind):
- to see the flop
- to limp in for cheap in late position.

Call (one or more raise):
- to see the flop, if on a potentially winning hand
- to slow-play a big hand
- to play a low pocket pair, looking for trips
- to play suited connectors
- to play a lesser hand which may come good on the flop.

Raise (low):
- to reduce, but not to eliminate, opponents
- to boost the pot, assuming you'll win it.

Raise (high), preferably in late position:
- to steal the blinds
- if on a big hand against 'calling-stations'.

Fold:
- to minimise losses, if you think you're beaten (unless on the big blind and flop can be seen for free).

Post-flop

Check:
- to slow-play a strong hand
- to await a bet, so you can raise and win or steal the pot
- to try to see the turn for free
- in late position with losing hole cards when no-one has bet.

Bet (small):
- to 'announce' a hand and have players call or raise
- to feel out opponents (if on, say, a middling pair)
- to attempt to neutralise a potentially large bet from an opponent – a small bet can sometimes disarm them (but they may, of course, still raise)
- in late position to boost the pot, if on a winning hand
- in late position to steal the pot if you sense weakness in your opponents.

Bet (large):
- to take down the pot with a winning hand
- to steal the pot, if on a bluff
- to reduce or eliminate opponents (if, say, on a high pair and the flop shows a potential flush or straight draw).

Raise (small):
- to boost the pot, assuming an eventual win
- to test opponents' mettle (not for the faint of heart – you may get re-raised)
- in late position to reduce number of opponents
- in late position to bluff opponents.

Raise (large):
- to shut down the hand (if you've one or more overpairs and don't want fourth street to fill potential flushes or straights)
- in late position to take down or maximise the pot if on a winning hand
- in late position to steal the pot, if on a bluff
- in late position to bluff an opponent who you suspect has a winning hand
- in late position to out-bluff a bluffer.

Call:
- to slow-play a powerful hand
- if four cards to a flush or heart draw (if bet is still affordable).

Fold:
- to minimise losses if a bet has been made and you are beaten.

On the Turn

Check:
- to see 'fifth street' for free (if on a drawing hand)
- if you've losing hole cards
- to slow-play a winning hand, especially if you've the nuts
- to gain an extra bet from your opponent, whether you raise or call.

Bet (small):
- to boost the pot, if on a winning hand

- to disguise a monster hand (a small bet is more likely to be called)
- to attempt to steal the pot if you sense weakness in your opponents
- to attempt to neutralise a potentially large bet from an opponent – a small bet will sometimes disarm them (but they may still raise).

Bet (large):
- to take down or maximise the pot with a winning hand
- to steal the pot, if on a bluff
- to reduce or eliminate opponents (say, if you've made a medium heart flush and don't want to see a fourth heart hit the board).

Raise (small):
- to maximise the pot if on a winning hand
- to boost the pot, assuming an eventual win
- to bluff out an opponent.

Raise (large):
- to maximise the pot if on a winning hand (and you suspect others have good but lesser hands)
- to steal the pot, if on a bluff
- to bluff out an opponent whom you suspect of holding a winning hand
- to out-bluff a bluffer.

Call:
- to slow-play a powerful hand (trips, straight, flush, quads) if on a draw (but *only* if the bet is still cheap).

Fold:
- to minimize losses if a bet has been made and you are beaten.

On the River

Check:
- if you've losing hole cards (you may still be able to raise if on a bluff)
- to slow-play a winning hand – only if you think your opponent(s) will bet.

Bet (small or large):
- even if you suspect you're losing, it's nearly always better to bet or raise rather than check on the river (whether winning, bluffing or semi-bluffing), especially if in late position.
- Aggression at the endgame of a hand wins pots. Consistent aggression throughout the hand (even or especially if bluffing) is more likely to succeed. *Do not* bluff or semi-bluff a player who has raised before the flop or is a calling station playing unusually in the hand.

Raise (small or large), with the best hand, though how much you raise your opponent(s) is a measured judgement:
- to bluff weak opponent(s)
- to outbluff a bluffer (who can be bluffed).

Fold:
- to surrender the hand (and your money). Once it's in the pot, it's no longer yours. Don't, as they say, throw good money after bad.

✻

Of course, every hand in Hold'em is near unique. You must adapt your betting skills to and for every new situation at every new point of every Hold'em hand. Only when confronting your opponent(s) across the green baize – whether real or virtual – will your poker instincts take over and tell you how much to charge them down with, whether to bluff them out of the pot or maximise your winnings. Have fun with numbers and, remember, a caller is rarely a winner. Raise away!

Bad Beats

You will, more often than you should, endure 'bad' as opposed to legitimate beats in Hold'em. Here's an example. You flopped the top straight and raised Mr Lucky hoping to shut down the hand. He, feeling as lucky as his name, re-raised. Scenting easy money, you re-raise him all in. He calls with top pair and top kicker.

You   Mr Lucky

The Flop:

The Wit of Poker

'Better one day as a lion than a lifetime as a lamb' was the motto of 1982 World Champion Jack Straus, who was also fond of saying, 'If the Lord had meant you to hold on to money, he'd have made it with handles on.' Jack was down to one chip at one point in the 1982 WSOP that he wound up winning, giving rise to the phrase: '[All you need is] a chip and a chair.'

Jack once made one of the most elegant bluffs ever, which also shows how witty a game poker can often be. In the words of Al Alvarez, in *The Biggest Game in Town*:

At No Limit Hold'em, Straus was dealt 7-2 offsuit, the worst hand in the deck. But he was 'on a rush', so he raised anyway, and only one other player stayed with him. The flop was dealt: 7-3-3-, giving Jack two pairs. He bet again, but as he did so he saw his opponent's hand reach quickly for his chips, and he knew he had made a mistake. The other guy, Jack realised, had a big pair in the hole (it was in fact two jacks); with great confidence, he raised Jack's $5,000. At that point, the logical move was to fold, since Jack was certain he was beaten and only a bluff could save him. But he called, thereby sowing doubt in the other player's mind.

The dealer turned over the fourth card: a deuce. It paired Jack's second hole card, but did not improve his hand, since there was already a communal pair of threes on the board. In other words, he knew he was still losing. Without hesitating, Jack bet $18,000. There was a long, long silence while the other man considered the implications of the bet. Then Jack leaned forward, smiling his most charming, lop-sided smile. 'I'll tell you what,' he said. 'You give me one of those little twenty-five-dollar

> *chips of yours, and you can see either of my cards, whichever you choose.' Another silence. Finally, the man tossed over a yellow-and-green chip and pointed to one of the cards in front of Jack. Jack turned it over: a deuce. Another long silence. The only logical explanation for Jack's offer was that the two cards in front of him were the same, so the flop gave him a full house of deuces. The other man folded his winning hand.*
>
> *'It was just a matter of simple psychology,' Straus said later. But Alvarez thought it was a lot more than that. 'It wasn't just simple psychology, nor was it merely a matter of bluff. It was a play in the true sense: a kind of wit, stylish, elegant and full of imagination.'*

Since he's all in, you go 'on your backs' and turn your cards face up. Mr Lucky sighs. 'I thought you were bluffing,' he mumbles, as if to undercut the realisation that he's been completely outplayed. Then fourth and fifth street are dealt:

The Board:

Unbelievable? He had 11 possible outs from forty-five cards (two jacks, three aces, three 8s and three 9s), but needed two of them to turn up and *both* of them did. Well, it happens sooner or later to everyone. So remember:

1. Poker would not be poker without bad beats.
2. Bad beats can throw even the most experienced

Player Profile:

Chip Reese

Originally from Dayton, Ohio, David E. 'Chip' Reese started playing poker during childhood but it was while studying economics at Dartmouth College, New Hampshire, that he earned his first real taste of success. In fact, his play so dominated the campus that on his graduation the college poker room was renamed the 'David E. Reese Memorial Cardroom' in his honour. Reese next planned to attend Stanford Law School but stopped off in Las Vegas on his way to enrol. One $60,000 tournament win later and he knew that he'd never make it to Stanford. Widely considered the best high stakes cash game player in the world today, Reese has two WSOP bracelets from winning Seven Card Stud events in 1978 and 1982. His chapter in Doyle Brunson's original *Super System* is still considered the best text ever compiled on Seven Card Stud. 'He's the best Seven Card Stud player I ever played with,' Brunson said of Reese in the book, also crediting him with being 'one of the two finest young all-round players in the world' at the time (the other was 1978 WSOP Champ Bobby Baldwin). Chip Reese was inducted into Binion's Hall of Fame in 1991 at the age of forty and remains the youngest living Hall-of-Famer.

players off their game. After suffering a bad beat, take a moment to 'reconfigure' your playing qualities in your mind, before entering a new hand or a new game (especially a higher-stakes game). Bad beat victims are the surest candidates to go 'on tilt', or start playing badly. Do not let one bad beat evolve into a cash haemorrhage via undisciplined, impatient, loose play.

3. It hurts for a while, but take consolation in the fact that you had a 'bad' as opposed to a 'good' beat. You played the hand correctly and your opponent got lucky. It's better than getting outplayed.

4. Everyone has bad beats and bad-beat stories – and bad-beat stories, unless exceptionally well told, are predictably boring.

Here are some of the less tedious ones, from the World Series of Poker:

Brent Carter v Barbara Enright, WSOP $10,000 Main Event, Day 4, 1995

Still the only woman to have made the final table in the WSOP's Main Event, Barbara Enright would have finished higher than fifth – maybe even have won it – were it not for the following bad beat against a fellow pro called Brent Carter.

Everybody had passed round to Barbara in the big blind with pocket eights, Carter having completed the small blind with a 6-3. So Barbara moves all in – and Carter calls, weirdly risking all of his chips.

Carter flops both a 6 and a 3 for two pair. Now that's when a bad call turns into a bad beat.

John Shipley v Phil Ivey, WSOP $10,000 Main Event, Day 3, 2002

With fewer than 100 players left, England's John Shipley and top pro Phil Ivey both see a flop of A-3-4. Each bets more than $130,000, putting Shipley all in. Ivey shows pocket 3s for trips, Shipley turns over A-K for a strong pair of aces.

At this point Ivey is a 50–1 favourite. The turn brings another ace, giving Shipley trip aces but Ivey a full house. Then the river brings the last ace in the deck, giving Shipley quads – a 989–1 shot. Ivey never fully recovers, and finishes twenty-third, while Shipley continues his roll all the way to the final table.

Robert Varkonyi v Phil Hellmuth Jr, WSOP $10,000 Main Event, Day 3, 2002

With sixty players left, and blinds at $1,200–$2,400 (+ $400 ante), Varkonyi opens the betting from early position for $8,000 with Q♣-10♣. Holding A♥-K♥, Hellmuth re-raises $17,000 more from the small blind. With a cry of 'I'm all in', Varkonyi shoves in his remaining $98,000. Hellmuth thinks long and hard, finally calling the bet. Varkonyi pairs his queen, and 1989 world champ Phil Hellmuth is sent packing.

This bad beat gets worse when Hellmuth later vows on TV to shave his head if Varkonyi winds up winning the tournament. Varkonyi does – again with Q-10 – and global TV licks its lips as the clippers are duly applied to Hellmuth's handsome head of hair.

Chris Moneymaker v Humberto Brenes, WSOP $10,000 Main Event, Day 4, 2003

After getting heads up, and seeing a flop of K-9-2, Brenes makes a huge bet of $70,000. Moneymaker studies him through his mirrored sunglasses, and shouts 'I raise you all your chips' – $120,000. Wagging his finger at the unfortunate Moneymaker, a delighted Brenes immediately says, 'I call.' Moneymaker turns over pocket 8s, Brenes pocket aces.

Brenes is an 11–1 favourite, more when the flop brings rags. But the turn brings 8♣. Moneymaker knocks out Brenes, and zooms to a chip lead of $1.5 million by the end of Day 4. But he wasn't done yet with inflicting Bad Beats (see pp. 112–13) …

Winning Percentages

Okay, that's enough fun for this chapter. Now it's time to study some form. You can't be expected to memorise these; but scan them long enough, and you'll get a feel for which hands to play, and which to fold.

Pocket Pairs: Winning Percentages

No. of players:	2	3	4	7	10
A-A	88%	76%	68%	44%	34%
K-K	85%	72%	63%	39%	30%
Q-Q	82%	68%	58%	34%	26%

J-J	79%	64%	54%	30%	22%
10-10	77%	60%	50%	27%	20%
9-9	74%	56%	46%	25%	18%
8-8	71%	52%	43%	23%	16%
7-7	68%	48%	39%	21%	14%
6-6	65%	45%	36%	20%	13%
5-5	63%	43%	33%	19%	12%
4-4	60%	40%	30%	17%	11%
3-3	57%	37%	26%	16%	10%
2-2	55%	34%	22%	15%	10%

No hand, in other words, is infallible. I cannot print the things I've heard when pocket aces have wound up getting beaten – which happens more often than you'd expect. But that doesn't mean you shouldn't bet them – and bet them big. It's the only time, before the flop, that you *know* you're holding the best hand. The question is how to convert it into the most money.

Note also how the value of your hand increases dramatically with fewer players at the table.

All of the following tables are approximate, and vary slightly from manual to manual. These are rough guides, compiled with the help of an expert. The mathematics may be over your head – as, much of the time, it's over mine – but they'll give you a sense of the relative strengths of Hold'em hands at each stage of the game and its betting rounds. Only by playing a lot will you find these charts turning into instinctive, if well-calibrated, gut feelings – which the poker gods may then, of course, choose to defy.

This first one explains the chances of your starting hands standing up as the five communal cards come into play. Those that follow are more complex variations on the same theme, at the three post-flop stages.

Approximate Percentage Chance of Winning of Pre-flop Starting Hands

Top pair v smaller pair	e.g. A♠-A♥ v K♦-K♣ or J♥-J♦ v 5♣-5♠	= 80%–20%
Top pair v suited connector	e.g. K♠-K♣ v 9♥-10♥ or Q♥-Q♠ v 3♣-4♣	= 80%–20%
Top pair v high suited connector	e.g. A♠-A♦ v K♣-Q♣ or Q♥-Q♣ v J♠-10♠	= 83%–17%
Top pair v low–medium suited connectors	e.g. K♥-K♣ v 6♠-7♠ or Q♦-Q♠ v 6♥-5♥	= 77%–33%
Top pair v off-suit connectors	e.g. K♠-K♣ v 8♥-9♦ or J♥-J♦ v 2♠-3♣	= 80%–20%
Top pair v off-suit connectors (where pair includes suited overcard(s))	e.g. A♠-A♥ v K♥-Q♠ or Q♦-Q♣ v 9♣-10♦	= 88%–12%
Top pair v lower cards off-suit	e.g. A♥-A♦ v 2♠-10♦	= 85%–15%
Top pair v lower cards off-suit (where pair includes suited overcard(s))	e.g. A♠-A♥ v 2♠-10♥	= 88%–12%

Top pair v lower cards off-suit (where lower cards have straight potential)	e.g. K♠-K♥ v 4♦-8♣ = 81%–19%
Top pair v off-suit high card (of same denomination + kicker)	e.g. A♠-A♥ v A♦-K♣ = 92%–8% or J♥-J♣ v J♠-10♦
Top pair v suited high card (of same denomination + kicker)	e.g. A♠-A♥ v A♣-K♣ = 86%–14% or J♥-J♣ v J♠-10♠

The underdog in any pre-flop stand-off against a high pair, more often than not, has around a 1 in 5 chance of winning.

Suited overcards v smaller pair	e.g. Q♥-J♥ v 8♦-8♣ = 52%–48% or A♠-Q♠ v 10♦-10♣
Off-suit overcards v smaller pair	e.g. K♥-10♦ v 7♦-7♣ = 56%–44% or A♠-J♣ v 9♥-9♦
Suited overcards v low pair	e.g. A♥-Q♥ v 5♦-5♣ = 48%–52% or J♠-10♠ v 4♦-4♥
Off-suit overcards v low pair	e.g. A♣-K♦ v 3♥-3♠ = 48%–52% or Q♦-10♠ v 2♥-2♣

Off-suit over-cards v off-suit lower cards (of which one is same denomination)	e.g. A♠-K♥ v A♦-9♣ or J♣-10♦ v J♥-9♠	= 70%–30%
Suited overcards v suited lower cards (of which one is same denomination)	e.g A♥-Q♥ v Q♦-2♦ or K♣-10♣ v 10♦-5♦	= 70%–30%
Off-suit over-cards v suited lower cards (of which one is same denomination)	e.g. A♣-K♦ v A♥-8♥ or Q♥-J♠ v J♣-4♣	= 70%–30%
Suited overcards v off-suit lower cards (of which one is same denomination)	e.g. K♦-J♦ v J♠-3♥ or Q♥-J♠ v J♣-4♣	= 75%–25%

So remember that a small pair v overcards – i.e. two unpaired cards both higher than the pair – is a 'coin-flip', or close to 50–50, most of the time.

So-called 'dominated hands' have only a one in three chance of coming good against cards of which one is the same and one higher.

Percentage Chance of Drawing Winning Hands on Turn

On Flop	Winning Hand	Outs	%	Odds
Pocket pair J♠-J♥-x-x-x	Three of a kind J♠-J♥-x-x-J♦	2	4.3	22.5–1
Two pair J♠-J♥-8♦-8♣-x	Full house J♠-J♥-J♦-8♦-8♣	4	8.5	10.8–1
Inside straight 7-8-x-10-J	Straight 7-8-9-10-J	4	8.5	10.8–1
Pair J♠-J♥-8♦-x-x	Three of a kind J♠-J♥-8♦-J♦-x or two pairs J♠-J♥-8♦-8♣-x	5	10.6	8.4–1
Overcards A-J (v, e.g. 8-8)	Top Pair A-J-x-A-x	6	12.8	6.8–1
Straight draw 5-6-7-8-x	Straight 5-6-7-8-9	8	17	4.9–1
Flush draw A♠-K♠-8♠-6♠-x	Flush A♠-K♠-8♠-6♠-2♠	9	19.1	4.2–1
Three of a kind J♠-J♥-J♦-6♠-x	Four of a kind J♠-J♥-J♦-6♠-J♣ or full house J♠-J♥-J♦-6♠-6♥	10	21.3	3.7–1
Straight flush draw K♠-Q♠-J♠-10♠-x	Straight K♠-Q♠-J♠-10♠-9♦ or flush K♠-Q♠-J♠-10♠-2♠	15	31.9	2.1–1

Percentage Chance of Drawing Winning Hands on River

On Flop	Winning Hand	Outs	%	Odds
Pocket pair J♠-J♥-x-x-x	Three of a kind J♠- J♥-x-x-J♦	2	4.3	22–1
Two pair J♠-J♥-8♦-8♣-x	Full house J♠-J♥-8♦-8♣-J♦	4	8.7	10.5–1
Inside straight 7-8-x-10-J	Straight 7-8-9-10-J	4	8.7	10.5–1
Pair J♠-J♥-8♦-x-x	Three of a kind J♠-J♥-8♦-x-J♦ or two pairs J♠-J♥-8♦-x-8♣	5	10.9	8.2–1
Overcards A-J (v, e.g. 8-8)	Top Pair A-J-x-x-A	6	13	6.7–1
Straight draw 5-6-7-8-x	Straight 5-6-7-8-9	8	17.4	4.8–1
Flush draw A♠-K♠-8♠-6♠-x	Flush A♠-K♠-8♠-6♠-2♠	9	19.6	4.1–1
Three of a kind J♠-J♥-J♦-6♠-x	Four of a kind J♠-J♥-J♦-6♠-J♣ or full house J♠-J♥-J♦-6♠-6♥	10	21.7	3.6–1
Straight flush draw K♠-Q♠-J♠-10♠-x	Straight K♠-Q♠-J♠-10♠-9♦ or flush K♠-Q♠-J♠-10♠-2♠	15	32.6	2.1–1

Percentage Chance of Drawing Winning Hands on Turn or River

On Flop	Winning Hand	Outs	%	Odds
Pocket pair J♠-J♥-x-x-x	Three of a kind J♠-J♥-x-x-J♦	2	8.4	10.9–1
Two pair J♠-J♥-8♦-8♣-x	Full house J♠-J♥-J♦-8♦-8♣	4	16.5	5.1–1
Inside straight 7-8-x-10-J	Straight 7-8-9-10-J	4	16.5	5.1–1
Pair J♠-J♥-8♦-x-x	Three of a kind J♠-J♥-8♦-J♦-x or two pairs J♠-J♥-8♦-8♣-x	5	20.3	3.9–1
Overcards A-J (v, e.g. 8-8)	Top Pair A-J-x-A-x	6	24.1	3.1–1
Straight draw 5-6-7-8-x	Straight 5-6-7-8-9	8	31.5	2.2–1
Flush draw A♠-K♠-8♠-6♠-x	Flush A♠-K♠-8♠-6♠-2♠	9	35	1.9–1
Three of a kind J♠-J♥-J♦-6♠-x	Four of a kind J♠-J♥-J♦-6♠-J♣ or full house J♠-J♥-J♦-6♠-6♥	10	38.4	1.6–1
Straight flush draw K♠-Q♠-J♠-10♠-x	Straight K♠-Q♠-J♠-10♠-9♦ or flush K♠-Q♠-J♠-10♠-2♠	15	54.1	0.8–1

5

Dealer's Choice

Once you've mastered the odds, get to know the game's different betting structures. There are three kinds in poker: limit, pot limit and no limit.

Limit

In limit poker, all bets are fixed. A £10–£20 game would have a small blind of £5 and a big blind of £10, which is therefore the minimum bet to come in. After the flop, the minimum *and maximum* bet or raise remains in units of £10, followed by £20 after the turn and the river. In limit games, the number of raises allowed is usually limited to (or 'capped' at) three per round of betting.

Limit poker is the best real-money arena for a beginner to start learning how to play. Your losses per hand are regulated; but then so are your winnings. The disadvantage is that it is very difficult, in this type of

poker, to bet or raise – let alone bluff – other players out
of the pot.

Pot Limit

In pot-limit poker, players can bet the size of the pot, or
raise 'the max' (including their call). But beware: after
multiple raises, the pot will escalate rapidly. Having made
a pre-flop call of £5, you may well find yourself staring
down the barrel of a three-figure shoot-out by fifth street.

This is why players who like to push their luck (and
their skill) scoff at limit games. There's more subtlety,
more opportunity to bluff, and to make a mint in a game
where the pots, to use a favourite phrase of the legendary
'Amarillo Slim' Preston's, are 'higher than a dawg can
jump over'.

No Limit

That's why big-money players prefer no-limit poker, in
which players can at any time bet as much as they like, up
to going 'all in', or betting every chip they have in front of
them. If limit poker is a science, no-limit poker is an art.
This is poker at its most deadly pure – and dangerously
lucrative. It's not for nothing that the WSOP Main Event
is a No-Limit Hold'em Championship.

The best no-limit players have an almost preternatural
ability to work out what their opponents are holding.
They gauge their hands by watching how they bet. This is
what the great Doyle 'Texas Dolly' Brunson means when

Barry Greenstein

Nicknamed 'The Robin Hood of Poker' because he donates all of his tournament winnings to charity, Greenstein grew up in Chicago and earned a PhD in mathematics from the University of Illinois. He famously won two million-dollar tournaments in 2003: Larry Flynt's 'Million Dollar Stud' Poker Challenge Cup at the Hustler Casino in LA and the Jack Binion World Poker Open Championship in Tunica, Mississippi. He has two WSOP gold bracelets, won at the 2004 $5,000 No-Limit Deuce-to-Seven Draw event and the $2,000 No-Limit Hold'em event in 2005. Greenstein was invited to write a chapter for Doyle Brunson's *Super System 2*, but when the chapter ran over 100 pages, he turned it into his own tournament strategy guide, *Ace on the River*, for which Brunson wrote the foreword. Greenstein's website barrygreenstein.com contains details of the numerous tournaments he arranges as charity fundraisers, alongside a controversial and fascinating 'Player Analysis' section in which he gives the world's most celebrated players individual ratings for aggressiveness, looseness and 'steam control' as well as limit, no-limit, and tournament play. Many revealing first-person insights are to be found there.

he says he can play entire hands blind – without even looking at his hole cards – when his powers of perception are in full flow. Hence one of poker's most important maxims: as you get to know the players around you at the table, whether or not you've played with them before, always 'play the player, not the cards'.

There is a school of thought that you should never play for more than you can afford to lose. 'Scared money always loses' is wise advice that most self-styled card sharps, myself included, have at some point failed to heed. When you've begun to feel comfortable at the £10–£20 limit table, maybe even 'got ahead' (started making a profit), your natural instinct will be to graduate to the £20–£40 table – where the competition will, by definition, be of a higher standard, as will the bankrolls. Hence another golden rule, part of the seminal art of 'bankroll management': always stay within your comfort zone.

But I also believe it's only when you've lost more than you can afford that you come to understand the real danger of the game, and get a better feel for it. That's not an encouragement to quit your job, take out a second mortgage and hot-foot it to Vegas, though some have (while others have never come back). It's just part of any grizzled player's learning curve to analyse their losses, far more than their big wins, and understand why they let themselves get beat.

Strategy

Whatever kind of Hold'em game you're in, experienced players will usually raise pre-flop with a high pocket pair or ace-suited to prevent people in later position 'limping in' with lesser hands that may come good on the flop. Calling these raises with lesser hands in the hope of a helpful flop will all depend on your skills of perception: your reading of the other players, along with what position you're in, how much has been raised, how many chips you have relative to them – and so on. The subtleties of the betting cycles in poker are infinite.

When you're playing in person, as opposed to online, every facial tic, each fleeting expression, every body movement, a player's posture, their eyes – if not hidden by trademark dark eyewear – should clue you into their game. Observation. Concentration. And aggression.

Consider two players, an Englishman holding A♠-Q♠, an American with 9♥-9♦. The Englishman bets, to protect his strong hand pre-flop, but runs into the Yank, who raises. The remaining players scatter. The Englishman calls the raise. The flops comes: 2♠-9♠-Q♥.

The Englishman now believes he has a strong hand, perhaps the best: top pair with the highest available kicker. He bets. But again he runs into the American, who raises with three of a kind. Since the Englishman is also four-to-a-flush, he calls. Fourth Street comes: J♠.

The Englishman has now made his flush (A♠-Q♠-J♠-9♠-2♠) and bets big. What does the Yank do? It depends on his perceptions of the Englishman's hand. He may be 'representing' a flush or a straight at fourth street: 2♠-9♠-Q♥-J♠. Does the American believe the Englishman actually holds the winning flush? Does he lay down his own trips? What are his outs if the Englishman is holding 8-10 or 10-K (a straight) or five spades (as, in fact, is the case)? Being a 'loose', aggressive player – reluctant to lay

down his trip nines – even believing the Englishman is
bluffing, the American calls. A wise call?

Well, he has ten outs: three jacks or three queens (as far
as he knows) to pair the board and give him a full house,
ditto three 2s, or the fourth nine. The pot is offering him
decent odds, and the river brings ... a Q♣. The Englishman still has his flush (the better hand than three of a kind
– always the best five cards, remember) while the American has made his boat – a full house, nines full of queens
(9-9-9-Q-Q) – and scoops a big pot.

It's second-best hands like these that can lose you a lot
of money playing poker. Be careful not to over-bet a
strong hand when suckering players in. If you're holding
A-J and the flop comes J-J-7, it would be perfectly reasonable to check your trips, watching out for potential
flushes, calling your opponents' bets to keep them in the
hand. But with each new card emerging, the best hand is
changing, and so endangered. If fourth street brings a Q
and another player has J-Q, you are suddenly caught in
your own carefully laid trap – and it will cost you.

Just as having the second-best hand is pricey, so the
hand you think second worst may surprise you; when the
bet is checked to you at fifth street, you bet ... and your
opponent folds. Equally, you may call an opponent and
be surprised to find their hand is less strong than you
expected.

That's why it's worth making small bets early on, especially in a tournament with rising blinds (where, over
time, the rounds of betting become progressively more
expensive). You must 'feel out' your opponents, get to
know their styles of play, which hands they'll bet with,
which hands they'll bluff with.

Watch their expressions, their hands hovering near their chips. And if you're online, pay close attention to their reaction times. It is absolutely possible to 'read' your opponents' poker character via their betting patterns, even if they're in Anchorage or Shanghai or Auckland (at a random sample) and represented by a faceless cyber-avatar.

Poker is not for the faint-hearted. At its best, the game is played with energy, powerful concentration, endless aggression and the intangible quality the great players know as 'heart'. A caller (or 'calling-station') is not a winner. Raising is what wins you pots. But it takes heart to raise, to bluff a player out of a legitimately powerful hand by going all in on the river. Ask yourself: do you have 'heart'?

Women Players

Many women do. More than you might think – if you're a man. Beyond the actress Jennifer Tilly, who won an event at the 2005 WSOP, Annie Duke and Jennifer Harman (see panels, pp. 26 and 50) are but two of the top professional players in today's game, as well as England's own Lucy Rokash.

Poker is one of the sports at which men and women compete on utterly equal terms – which is why some of the top female pros refuse to take part in the annual women's events, preferring to play as a human being in the other events.

But I don't expect you to take my word for it. I asked the Moll from *Big Deal*, American novelist Cindy Blake, to give us her own perspective:

Dave 'Devilfish' Ulliot

A native of Hull, Ullliott started out as a jeweller and pawn-broker playing cash games on the side. After becoming a dominating presence at the Victoria Casino in London, he began playing in Vegas in 1996 and soon made a name for himself, winning the 1997 WSOP Pot-Limit Omaha event. Nicknamed after a poisonous fish that can be lethal if not cooked properly, Ulliott became famous in Britain after winning the inaugural *Late Night Poker* series, and world-renowned after winning the $10,000 No-Limit Hold'em Jack Binion World Poker Open in Tunica, Mississippi in 2003, a WPT event. With over $3 million in tournament winnings, the Devilfish is the most successful British tournament player on the international circuit. 'I started off by losing plenty of money,' Ulliott says. 'Now, if there's a game, I don't even get invited.' An online representative of both ultimatepoker.com and ultimatebet.com, Ulliott's website thedevilfish.com sells his DVDs, personalised chips, poker tables and card shufflers.

It's getting harder to be a female poker player – because there are more female poker players around. In the good old days, when casinos were de facto men's clubs, the rare appearance of a woman sitting at the poker tables brought with it the male assumption that this was a hapless poker virgin who didn't know what she was doing. And any time people make assumptions like that at a poker table, they're bound to lose.

Which meant we women had an advantage and could use two simple strategies to exploit it. Either we played really tight for the first hour, thus reinforcing the male stereotype that women don't bluff – and then, of course, bluff like mad. Or we could act like a ditzy blonde/brunette/redhead for the first hour – and then play like a rock. It helped, whichever strategy we used, to dress seductively. Cleavage and short skirts worked both as a distraction and a reinforcement of the 'not serious poker player' image.

Now that there are so many highly accomplished women playing in casinos and tournaments, however, the old methods are effectively useless. Men have learned not to fall for the obvious tricks. But we still have one ace up our sleeves. Men hate losing to women. It doesn't matter how much they may respect and admire our ability at the tables, the average poker-playing man can't stand it if we take his money. And this makes for another good female strategy.

Instead of looking for the 'sucker' at the table, a woman should look for the alpha male. The one who comes across as macho, who makes comments about a woman being there, who displays his ego. And if she has a chance to go one-on-one in any pot with him, she should take it. He'll stay in when he shouldn't. His pride

won't let him fold. Even if he wins a few of these con-
tests, she should stick with the strategy. He'll be so full
of himself, he'll forget the basics. And if he loses a few
pots to her he'll be so desperate to win the next ones,
he'll go on tilt.

Any woman thinking of taking up poker has to learn
not to be riled by sexist comments and male condescen-
sion, but to use them to her advantage. Because men
aren't used to women being their equals in what is effectively a sport, they can often be cowed by a woman who
bets aggressively from the start. Somewhere in most
male brains lurks the idea that women are more careful
about money and less prone to risk than they are, so
strong female play is often rewarded. In fact, most
women poker players prefer to play against men rather
than women. It's harder to fool a fellow female; and
harder to read them than it is to read a man.

There are thousands of reasons for a woman to start
playing poker. One of the best ones, if she has ever
wanted revenge on the male species, is to see the look on
a man's face when she check-raises.

Who am I to argue with that?

6

Home Games, Tournaments and Online Play

Texas Hold'em, to give the game its full name, is not the only poker game, just the most popular – especially at the highest levels, being the game played to decide the world title. Five-card draw, as seen in most western movies, is rarely played these days. The most popular poker games, apart from Hold'em, are stud, razz and Omaha.

In seven-card stud, each player is dealt three cards – two down, one up before the first betting round. Three more up cards follow to each player, with a betting round between each, before the final, seventh card, dealt down. This is the age-old game on which Hold'em is an ingenious variant, invented with the idea of allowing more people to play. Stud poker can also be played with five cards – one down, four up.

Razz is also called lowball, in which the worst hand wins. Some variations allow the 'wheel' – A, 2, 3, 4, 5 – to count as the lowest hand, even though it is a straight. Otherwise, the best low hand is A-2-3-4-6.

The rules of Omaha are the same as those of Hold'em, except that each player is dealt *four* cards, and must use two of them – no more, no less – in combination with three from the board. Omaha can also be played high-low, with the best and the worst hands sharing the pot. The low must usually be 'eight or better', which requires three of the communal cards to be an eight or lower; otherwise there is no low, and the high hand wins all.

Home Games

You will perhaps try some or all of these, with variations of your own – but, please, *no* wild cards – in the home game you establish with a few pals every Friday night. You'll likely play limit or pot limit (or half-pot limit) rather than no limit, which can be too expensive for such friendly social games. At pot limit you may choose to impose a maximum bet – maybe £100 – depending on the size of everyone's bankroll. No doubt you'll invent some wild and whacky poker variants of your own, and no doubt players will be better at some than others.

Which is why you'll probably play Dealer's Choice, or a round of the game favoured by each first dealer in turn. In these circumstances, it has to be said, Hold'em is not at its most thrilling. A round every so often, among maybe six or seven players, will suddenly seem rather tame after all the action generated by the other games. To play Hold'em properly, you need to play nothing else all evening.

Regulars should club together to buy a baize cloth, traditionally green, for reasons beyond the merely atmospheric. You'll find your tablecloth rather hard to shuffle on, and sticky when it comes to manipulating the cards, let alone riffling your chips. For chips you used to have to go to a big department store; now they can easily be bought online. If you want casino-quality cards, the kind you can put in the dishwasher, some casinos sell them second-hand; for most home games, however, the Waddington's decks sold by your local newsagent are fine.

It's normal to pay the host pro rata for laying on food and booze, but do remember that in the UK it is illegal for a poker host to charge table money.

The easiest way to run the game is for every player to start with a pre-agreed total in chips, and to draw the same amount again as and when they want or need to, with the clearest head keeping a written record of it all. (In one home game I have played in, each player who drew more chips had to place an item of cutlery beside their chips for each re-draw, so the other players could keep track of their cash status. 'I feel naked,' the short stacks would cry, 'without a spoon!') That way, at the end of the evening, the settling up should be straight-forward.

And you might even wind up playing 'Indian' or 'Apache' poker, now popularised on television as 'Blind Man's Buff' – the most absurd form of Hold'em, in which you're the only player *not* to know what cards you are holding, while you can see everyone else's hand. This dubious goal is achieved by picking up your cards without looking at them, and holding them face-out on your forehead, so that you can't see them but every other player can. And you can see theirs. If you must sink this low, ignore all the advice I've given you so far; just chuck in your money and hope for the best.

Casino Card Rooms

When you've conquered your home game, you may feel like trying your luck in a casino. But many people say they feel intimidated the minute they walk in, awed by the chandeliers and deep-pile carpets, stumbling to find the card room amid all the jangling slot machines and the manic yells of the craps and roulette players.

My advice would be to take your time, soak it all up, wander around a bit until you begin to feel at home before seeking out the card room. Once you get there, hang around on the rail a while, watching the action and getting the feel of the place. Usually there'll be a board indicating the games being played, and the size of the action, with the names of players on the waiting list to sit down. Study that board, decide the game and the level at which you'll feel most comfortable, then wander over to watch the action at that table.

As a rough guide, you should probably sit down with at least a hundred times the price of the small blinds, i.e. £200 in a £2–4 game, £500 in the £5–£10. But look around carefully and note how much each player has in front of him. Watch a few hands, to get a feel for the style of play. Is one player bullying every hand? Is someone else talking too much? It's all part of casino poker. Probably the best way to start in a casino is to enter a tournament; that way, you get to play with experienced players on limited liability.

Player Profile:

Gus Hansen

Originally from Copenhagen, Gustav ('Gus') Hansen was a world-class backgammon player before turning his attentions to poker. He exploded onto the poker scene via the televised WPT, on which he won two championships in the 2003 series – the Commerce LA Poker Classic and the Bellagio Poker Classic – and a third the following year – the Poker-stars Caribbean Adventure. In a game that combines formidable mathematical analysis with dangerous, often reckless plays, Hansen is one of the most original and entertaining players to have emerged onto the international tournament scene. Renowned for phenomenal, seemingly wild, bluffs, Hansen has argued that he's often weighing his own poor hand against his opponents'. When forced to flip over rags at showdowns early in his career, he was known to declare 'I have a Gus.' 'Let them think I'm lucky,' Hansen says. 'It helps me if people think I'm crazy because there's a rationale behind a lot of things I do. One of my strengths is that I definitely make mistakes that other solid players wouldn't make, but I also make plays they wouldn't dream about.'

In the UK casinos are clubs, and until recently operated a so-called 'twenty-four-hour rule' to prevent 'impulse gambling' – i.e. you could not play until at least twenty-four hours after you had joined (which cost nothing). Now that it has finally woken up to the huge revenues available from gambling, and tabled plans for Vegas-style casinos around Britain, the government has finally scrapped this and other such obsolete and uniquely British 'nanny-state' rules – but UK casinos are still pale shadows of those in the US.

Many UK casinos also have a dress code, often banning T-shirts, trainers, sometimes jeans and even baseball caps. Americans visiting Britain, needless to say, cannot believe we are still living quite so far back in the Dark Ages – even though the minimum legal age for casino gambling in Britain is a mere eighteen, compared to twenty-one in the United States.

Table Images and Tells

When playing with real people, rather than online, whether in a home game or a casino, you will want to establish a positive 'table image'. In a home game, you'll usually be playing with people you know well, who will already have a mental picture of the kind of player you are. So keep mixing up your play; act unpredictable; defy their preconceptions. Act, as always, aggressive. That's the way to wind up a regular winner.

So the following advice applies more to casinos, whether cash games or tournaments, where you're playing with people you've never met before (some of them, these days, people you may have seen playing on TV). Don't be awestruck. You want them to be awed by you.

You'll have seen on television that many players these days wear impenetrably dark glasses, caps, even hoods (like American pro Phil Laak, whose complete disappearance behind an enveloping hood earned him the nickname of 'Unabomber') in an attempt to give away as little as possible. Others hide behind their iPods, or other music systems, so be sure to look for them turning down the volume when they get a good hand.

Quite a few sport good luck charms of one sort or another, from pictures of their children to lucky fruit (like Johnny Chan's famous orange); many poker players are so superstitious that they won't change their clothes after a win. Don't let any of these distractions put you off. On the contrary, use them against your opponents and in your own favour.

At Hold'em, for instance, don't feel obliged to look at your hole cards as soon as they reach you. Look at them when it's your turn to bet. You may feel like you're slowing things up a bit, but don't let that bother you. As the cards are being dealt, it's much more important that you watch the *other* players as they receive their cards – scrutinise their expressions, look for the tiniest 'tells', or clues to the strength of their hand, in the way they respond to what they see. If they spot you doing this, so much the better. They'll put you down as an experienced player, who knows what he's doing. This way, you'll get what you want at the poker table: respect.

Players whose faces are known from TV get respect the minute they sit down. It can work both ways: players fear them, but they also want to beat them; or to go home saying that they lost to Dave 'Devilfish' Ulliott (see panel, p. 86). So don't treat these people with more respect than they deserve. You're the one trying to earn the respect – with the sharpness of your responses, and the bold style of your play.

Table image is an important factor in the balance of power at a poker table. If the other players mark you down as a calling-station, they're rarely going to call when you finally get a hand. That's why you have to take risks as often as you can summon the courage, earning the respect you deserve.

'Tells' can be as obvious as a player fiddling with his signet ring when he's bluffing, as in the David Mamet movie *House of Games*, or riffling his chips with his left hand when he's going to fold (as spotted by Chris Money-maker's father during the final table of the World Series Chris won). The pupils of some players' eyes are said to dilate when they see a high pair in the hole. This is why the top players stare at opponents, often for uncomfortably long periods, when considering their bet. They're looking for tiny give-away signs of strength or weakness.

But 'tells' are usually subtler than that – raising too quickly, for instance, with a strong hand, or too slowly with a weak one. Here we enter deeper realms of bluff and double-bluff, for the experienced player holding the nuts is going to take his time about betting, as a display of apparent indecision. All this will become easier with experience.

For further advice on this, read 'Mad' Mike Caro's *Book of Tells*.

Tournament Play

Bear in mind the one obvious difference between tournament and cash-game poker. If you lose all your money in a cash game, you can reach into your pocket for more, or you can go home. If you lose all your money in a tournament, you're already out the door.

The luck factor increases in a tournament – no one will win one without having won a few hands against the odds – but so does the skill factor. Plus experience. The key factors in tournament play are, as ever, aggression, patience and concentration. Reflect on your opponents' play as much as your own. Keep your eyes on theirs as they look at their hands. Be alert as to who is raising. Get to know these people and how they play poker. If you're not concentrating, someone else is – and benefiting as a result.

Some tournaments are 'freeze-outs', where you simply play until you've lost all your chips – or won everyone else's. Others have 'rebuys' – a period of time, usually an hour or two, when you can rebuy for the same as the entry fee if you lose all your chips or have less than a certain amount. Players like this, as of course it swells the prize pot.

Be prepared for wilder action during the 'rebuy' period than in normal 'freeze-out' play, especially from the short-stacks during the last few hands before the rebuys end. And be wary of the offer of an 'add-on' – the chance to buy more chips for the same amount when the rebuys end. I disapprove of these because they nullify all the skill displayed during the rebuy period. But if everyone else at

your table buys an 'add-on', it's hard not to join them.
Bear in mind, though, that if you're going to wind up
going all in, an add-on may not earn its keep by making
that much difference.

Early Stages

Play tight-aggressive. Raise or call only with big hands
(pocket pairs, A-K/Q/J/10) and limp in as much as possible with lesser hands. An ace with a middle/low kicker is
not a strong starting hand. Do not chase draws unless
you're odds-on to make your flush/straight – a higher
flush/straight than your opponent's – and on which you
can break them for 50 per cent or more of their chips.
Sometimes it's worth paying off players to find out what
they will and won't bet with ...

One way to lose tournaments is endlessly to chase
draws to the river. Chase draws only when hands are
checked to you or cheap to stay in. Then if your draw
comes off, be sure to profit from it. Do not chase dreams,
for you will rarely catch them.

Every hand has far more playability from late position.
A confident bet from a player in early position has far
more weight than from a player in late position. Shut
down pots with a big bet as soon as possible if your overpairs are likely to run into a straight or your straight into
a flush. If in doubt, bet bigger. Always bet on the river.
Call a final bet if pot odds are reasonable.

- A-A: Raise away. Push players to go all in. Whether
  you immediately go all in pre-flop or wait to sucker
  them post-flop is a judgement call – dependent on how

many callers you may or may not have.

- K-K: Raise away. Play this hand confidently. Just watch out for an ace on the board.
- A-K: You can be more or less confident of winning the hand with a big pre-flop raise but if you run into Q-Q or J-J, you'll have a 'coin-flip' on your hands.
- Q-Q/J-J/10-10: Be wary of going all in pre-flop unless you're short-stacked.
- A-9 (or lower kicker, unsuited): Play warily. Not as strong a hand as you might think it is, especially after half an hour of rags. Look for an over-pair with your kicker, then bet, then proceed with confident caution. Watch out for double-paired hands and draws.
- K-Q: A strong hand, and one of my favourites, but more vulnerable than it looks. Not worth calling big pre-flop raises, unless short stacked (when it could well be an all in hand). Watch out, as always, for that killer ace on the board.
- K-J/Q-J or lower: 'Paints', yes, but again not as strong a hand as it might look, especially after a dead half-hour. Worth limping in with in late position, but other-wise you should usually throw these hands away (however tempting they may seem) and, if the high card pairs on the flop, put it out of your head and get ready for the next hand.
- Low pocket pairs: Call (if the bet is reasonable) and hope to hit trips.
- Suited connectors: Call (if the bet is reasonable) and see if you hit a straight/flush draw. Always be aware that possible straight connectors (6-9) are far more powerful than hands which won't connect (2-8).

Middle Stages

Do not let yourself get short-stacked by just hanging in there, waiting for the nuts, or for other players to knock each other out. If you sit and wait, you'll soon find that you're the short-stack. Make moves from late position and be prepared to bluff if they don't come off. Bet confidently. Make your bluffs believable. Build a pot worth winning if you hold a winning hand. Suited hands have far more potency than unsuited. Be especially wary of being caught in raising matches between big hands, for you'll soon find yourself obliged to go all in. Hesitate before attacking the large stacks. If you yourself are the medium to short-stack, play every hand like it's your last.

Late Stages

Keep playing your way to the final table. You came here to win this thing, didn't you? Don't wait around to get in the money and find yourself short-stacked in the process. Go out to win. Steal blinds with big bets. As soon as you're ahead (i.e. chip-leader), sit back and watch the fireworks. Do some gentle bullying and stealing, sure, but let others knock each other out and don't get over-involved in hands that could hurt you. Use your pile to apply pressure to the short-stacks and always be ready for them to go all in. Chip away, but watch out for that all in re-raise. Bully the table but safeguard your stack. Chips not lost on loose calls are as significant as chips won against the odds. If you've a low pair and remaining players are short-stacked, put them all in (or nearly all in) anyway. Generally, it's not a good idea to go all in on a draw, unless you're absolutely forced to. Aggression, more often than not, pays off against short-stacks.

As you approach the final table, remember that the worst place to come is one off the money. That's called the 'bubble'. You'd rather have been the first player to be knocked out. You've played all those hours, perhaps all day, and beaten all those people, and you've got nothing to show for it. That's not a good rate of pay.

If and when you get to the 'heads-up', with just two of you left for the prize, remember that the values of the hole cards increase enormously. They have been increasing proportionally as the number of players at the table has decreased (see table, pp. 71–2). Any pair in the hole may well merit going all in, and the prize will probably be yours.

Select American Tournament Schedule

JAN: Jack Binion World Poker Open, Tunica, Mississippi

FEB: LA Poker Classic, Commerce Casino, Los Angeles

MAR: World Poker Challenge, Reno Hilton, Reno, Nevada

APR: Five-Star World Poker Classic, Bellagio, Las Vegas

MAY: Mirage Poker Showdown, Mirage, Las Vegas

JUNE–JULY: World Series of Poker, Rio, Las Vegas

JULY: Larry Flint's Grand Slam, Hustler Casino, Gardena, CA

AUG: Empire State Hold'em Championships, Turning Stone Resort, Verona, NY

SEPT: US Poker Championships, Trump Taj Mahal, Atlantic City, NJ

OCT: National Championship of Poker, Hollywood Park Casino, LA

NOV: World Poker Finals, Foxwoods, Mashantucket, CT
DEC: Turkey Shoot, Bicycle Casino, Bell Gardens, CA

Apart from the WSOP, this is a fairly random selection. For a full US tournament schedule, consult the American magazine Card Player or its website http://www.cardplayer.com/. The World Series of Poker (WSOP) now runs a tournament circuit as well as the World Poker Tour (WPT); details on their websites: http://www.worldseriesofpoker.com/ and http://www.worldpokertour.com/.

Select European Tournament Schedule

JAN: European Poker Tour, Copenhagen, Denmark
FEB: Bregenz Open, Casinos Austria, Bregenz
MAR: Vienna Spring Festival, Concord Card Casino, Vienna
APR: Lithuanian Championship, Olympic Casino, Vilnius
MAY: Paris Open, Aviation Club, Paris
JUNE: Summer Tournament, Grand Casino, Helsinki, Finland
JULY: Scottish Poker Championships, Gala Maybury, Edinburgh
AUG: European Open, Grosvenor Victoria Casino, London
SEPT: Barcelona Open, Casino Barcelona, Spain
OCT: Russian Poker Championships, Korona Casino, Moscow
NOV: Northern Lights Festival, Grosvenor Casino, Blackpool
DEC: Christmas Cracker Tournament, Rendezvous Casino, Brighton

This, too, is a pretty random selection. For a full European tournament schedule, consult the magazine Poker Europa or its website http://www.pokereuropa.net/. There is also a good tournament guide at the website of the Hendon Mob (see panel, p. 115), http://www.thehendonmob.com/.

Online Play

The first website to offer poker for real money was Planet Poker in 1998, swiftly followed the next year by Paradise Poker. By November 1999, Planet Poker had dealt its two-millionth hand; by February 2001 Paradise Poker had dealt its fifty millionth, doubled in a mere six months. Poker Stars launched in December 2001, Ladbrokes in May 2002.

So online poker is a comparatively young game, and a *huge* one, that is in a permanent state of development and refinement. There are plenty of good players out there, but even more weak ones (especially in the smaller-money games). So your job is to find the minnows by looking around the sites and sniffing our the 'dead money'.

You can start by playing for 'fun' money, renewable daily, until you feel comfortable with the web and its ways. Then you will want to graduate to the real-money games. Only when cash gets involved will you be able to refine your game and begin to play more expertly.

Playing online is a great way to learn the game, making your play ever more accurate, but it's not going to prepare you for the cut and thrust of a 'real' – or 'b&m', as in 'bricks-and-mortar' – poker table.

Online Poker Lingo

If you choose to banter with the other players online, you'll find they have their own code, usually abbreviations of phrases commonly exchanged at poker tables. Here are some basic examples:

nh = nice hand
vnh = very nice hand
gg = good going (i.e. well played)
wp = well played
ty = thank you (perhaps for one of the above messages)
str8 = straight, if you want to tell another player what you were holding, truthfully or not
lol = laugh out loud (if something weird has happened)
wtf = what the f***?

For a start, online poker is much quicker. You will have a fixed – and short – amount of time in which to make important decisions. This can sharpen your game, but it can also lead to mistakes – and make b&m poker seem very slow, the first few times you get to play it.

Online poker is less intimidating than the real thing. You're up against a bunch of faceless avatars, who aren't going to be trying to rile you as you weigh up your hand. Outside the entirely voluntary 'chat box' (see 'Lingo' box above), there is no talk at an online table. It can be a solitary business, playing in long-drawn-out online tournaments.

But at least you have minimised the distractions – the casino clatter etc. – which can give you the mother of all headaches in the real world of poker. Unless you choose to have an expert mentor at your shoulder, giving you advice – which is not, of course, allowed in all other forms of poker.

Online lobbies are far more helpful than their casino counterparts. Just by clicking a few buttons, before deciding which table to choose, you can learn the average pot size at any table, the number of players seeing the flop, how many hands they are playing per hour, the names of the players in each game (if you know your friends' online identities), how many are on the waiting list, and how many games of a particular limit are under way.

Once you get to your table, some of the important chores of card-room poker are done for you on the internet: figuring out the size of the pot, the size of the other players' stacks as well as your own – all of which are displayed for you, thus making it easier to calculate the pot odds as well as weighing up your standing in the global scheme of things.

Online Cashiers

Website cashiers accept money by credit card, US\$ cheque, bank draft or wire transfer. A credit card is usually the most convenient – and yes, most people do entrust theirs to these offshore squillionaires. Winnings will usually be refunded to the same credit card, or sometimes mailed by US\$ cheque. Websites also have daily maximum draws, something like \$600, but regular players can negotiate this upwards.

Player Profile:

Stu 'The Kid' Ungar

Widely considered to be the greatest No-Limit Hold'em player of all time, Ungar lived as he played: fast, loose and wild. He remains the only player in poker history to have won outright three WSOP No-Limit Hold'em championships, the first two back to back in 1981 and 1982, the third fifteen years later in 1997. Having earned his spurs as the greatest gin rummy player in his native New York, he moved to Vegas at twenty-three, where he soon ran out of gin opponents and moved on to poker. Nicknamed for his boyish looks, 'The Kid' had a near-unparalleled genius for cards, a photographic memory that could allegedly count a six-deck shoe, but squandered his winnings on sports betting, high living and the drug habit that eventually killed him. His uniquely brilliant, fascinating career is vividly recounted in the authoritative biography by Nolan Dalla and Peter Alson, *The Man Behind the Shades*.

Online dealers don't make mistakes, unlike some real dealers (who don't do it often, but it can cost you). The 'rake', or money you pay to play, is much smaller per hand than in a casino, leaving more for you to win. And the players, on the whole, are less experienced.

Online card rooms generally offer a wider choice of cash games and tournaments at all levels, with shorter (if any) waiting times, than casino card rooms.

Another of the great advantages of online poker is that you can get up and leave whenever you want to, especially when winning, without incurring the wrath of the other players.

One of the disadvantages of online poker is that it's generally much harder to bluff players out of a pot. It can be done; but the loss of the human interaction – the stares, the tells – makes it much tougher.

Remember also that some players hungry for action will be playing two, three, even four different tables at once. Unless you feel this good about yourself – in which case, I would suggest, it is time to take a break – you'll find that these players inevitably make mistakes, hurrying between one hand and the next in search of the biggest opportunities.

Online poker is available all day every day, all night every night. That may be its biggest appeal (and, for the easily addicted, drawback). Apart from the obvious advantage of being able to play at home, without having to travel across town to a casino or friend's home, even shave or get dressed if you can't be bothered, online poker can be very exciting and rewarding. But for most of those who have ever played with real people, it's a pale shadow of the real thing.

You will want to check the box that automatically posts your blinds, thus keeping the game moving; players who don't, and take a while to act, become unpopular. You would also be well advised to check the box offering to muck your hole cards if you lose; only when more experienced might you occasionally want to reveal them, maybe to show a bad beat, or the rest of the table that you actually do know what you are doing.

Online delays should, however, make you wary of the 'in turn' buttons allowing you to check, call or raise in advance of your turn. They're there to speed up the game, of which we're all in favour. But they're a tell to more experienced players; if someone raises ahead of you, what's more, and you suddenly want to fold, you can rue checking that 'call' box.

If the poker gods are really against you, you can even get disconnected in the middle of a hand. There are certain protections laid on by the authorities, but a disconnected player cannot finish a hand – distinctly annoying, and indeed costly, if you're holding the nuts.

Most online learners swiftly graduate to the tournament tables, where you can get a lot more top-class experience at lower levels of financial risk. Take your time in the lobby, and pick a tournament at the level where you feel comfortable. And remember the beauty of short-handed tournaments as a means of learning how to play. With five opponents rather than ten, let alone hundreds, you've a much better chance of winning!

On some websites, you can even order yourself a virtual cocktail, and/or packet of cigarettes. Weighing this detail alongside the permanent availability of poker – especially late at night, when the family is asleep – my

friend Patrick Marber, the writer of the movie *Closer* and
the classic poker play *Dealer's Choice*, once said to me:
'For us home-based writers, Tone, it's too good to be true.
And it's true.'

Top Dozen Poker Websites
(in no particular order)

Poker Stars @ http://www.pokerstars.com
Party Poker @ http://www.partypoker.com
Paradise Poker @ http://www.paradisepoker.com
Pacific Poker @ http://www.pacificpoker.com
Poker Room @ http://www.pokerroom.com
Inter Poker @ http://www.interpoker.com
Ladbrokes @ http://www.ladbrokespoker.com
William Hill @ http://www.williamhillpoker.com
Celebrity Poker @ http://www.celebpoker.com
Ultimate Bet @ http://www.ultimatebet.com
Full Tilt Poker @ http://www.fulltiltpoker.com
Doyle's Room @ http://www.doylesroom.com

Each of these has its merits; at Celebrity Poker, Doyle's
Room and Full Tilt you can play against 'name' players,
should you wish to be so bold. Shop around among them
for join-up bonuses, which are always varying. Try each
until you find the one where you feel comfortable. Start
with their 'play' money before graduating to 'real' money,
and opt for tournaments rather than cash games.

http://www.toppoker.org/poker-sites.html is a good site to
go to for current advice on offers and advice on styles of
play.

Finally, don't fret too much about nerds in Nissen huts

on Alaskan mountain sides ganging up on you; if you see any sign of collusion, or anything unusual, report it to the authorities, who are very vigilant. As for the authorities themselves, all based offshore, are they going to run off with all your money? As veteran cardroom manager Roy Houghton once said to me, 'The truth is they're making so much money they'd be mad to!'

7

The Road to the World Series

It's a great name for a gambler. And the genial answer to the question he's been asked a million times since May 2003 – 'Is that your real name?' – is a simple 'Yeah, sure!'

A former accountant from Nashville, Tennessee, Chris Moneymaker broke the mould by becoming the first World Champion to have won his $10,000 entry fee online, at the Poker Stars website, for a buck less than the $40 which has passed into poker history. By playing internet tournaments, Moneymaker turned just $39 into a $10,000 WSOP ticket. Then he turned that $10,000 into $2.5 million. It was the biggest parlay in the history of the game – until Greg 'Fossilman' Raymer improved on it the following year, winning $5 million for $160 through the same site.

In 2005, no fewer than 1,166 entrants to the WSOP's Main Event qualified (or won their $10,000 entry fee) via two- or three-figure satellites on Poker Stars – and 106 of them got in the money, winning some $2.5 million between them. Similarly, Party Poker boasted 641 qualifiers, of whom 106 wound up among the paid finishers, not least those who came fourth (with $2 million) and fifth (with $1.75 million) behind Joseph Hachem.

Back in 2003, Moneymaker's personal style throughout the Main Event was one of appealing unpretension. He made no bones about acting the amateur. By the third day he had no choice, when he found himself sitting at ESPN's featured table between two of the modern Vegas greats: two-time World Champ Johnny Chan and Howard 'The Professor' Lederer.

Watching Chan and Lederer raise and re-raise between them, Chris found himself awestruck to be playing alongside two of his heroes. But why was Johnny taking such a long time to bet? Only when Chan turned to Moneymaker and said, 'You know, it's on you, right?' did Chris realise that he himself was still in the hand. He had made the amateur mistake of being 'miles away' (see Items 1–4 in 'Beginner's Luck', p. 45).

After his pocket 8s knocked out Humberto Brenes' aces, thanks to an unlikely third 8 on the turn (as described on p. 71), he found a miraculous boat on the river to eliminate Phil Ivey, perhaps the most feared of the new generation of Vegas whizz-kids. Ivey started out with pocket 9s, and Moneymaker with A-Q. Moneymaker raised the blind, and Ivey, the 6–5 favourite, just called. The flop brings two queens, giving Moneymaker trips and suddenly making him a 12.5–1 favourite. But Phil stays in the hand, and is rewarded with a 9 on the turn, giving him a full house. Moneymaker makes a huge bet of $200,000, and Ivey announces he's all in. Moneymaker confidently calls, building the pot to over a million dollars. The cards go 'on their backs', and a chastened Moneymaker thinks he's out of the tournament. But the river brings one of his only four 'outs' – an ace, giving him a better full house, queens on aces.

So Moneymaker's story also became a legend of astonishing luck. Did he deserve to win the title? It is something players argue about to this day. But, hey, this is poker. If the other guy outdraws you, good luck to him. And there's nothing as important as how many chips are in front of any one player at any one time. By the end of the tournament's final day, Moneymaker had them all. And he, too, had shown heart.

The heads-up contest between Moneymaker and the fearsome Houston-based professional Sam Farha, which decided the title, has deservedly gone down in modern poker lore. It was not just that the internet amateur was taking on a popular and long-established pro, with a WSOP bracelet already to his name; it was the players' diverging styles: Moneymaker all iron and sinew, concealed behind baseball cap and wraparound shades to hide his tells; Farha relaxed and suave, coffee-housing like he was playing in a home game, taking drags on his trademark unlit cigarette – 'a pro,' in the words of *Time* magazine, 'whose cultivated look of disreputability is an artistic achievement'.

'Don't bluff me,' Farha told Moneymaker. 'Wait for the cards first.' But bluff him Chris did. With 4♠-7♠ in the hole, Chris watched the flop come 2-9-6♠. Farha had K-9. Holding top pair, he bet. Moneymaker called and the turn came 7♠. With an open-ended flush and straight draw, Moneymaker called Farha's bet. The river came 3♥, no help to either. But when Farha checked, Moneymaker bet everything he had. He well knew he'd lost the hand. There was no reason to go all in except on a stone-cold bluff. With equally cold professional logic, Farha folded the hand and with it, as it turned out, that year's world title. Soon it was all over, when Moneymaker flopped a full house against Farha's trip jacks.

Moneymaker proved to the exploding population of online players that one of their own could become a real-world champion, a feat repeated the following year when Greg 'Fossilman' Raymer won the 2004 Championship. The game would never be the same again.

Since these two won their bracelets, the golden symbol of a WSOP winner coveted by all players, it's been open season on the professionals. In 2005 Joe Hachem became the third unknown in succession to win the world title, giving further hope to amateurs everywhere. The only Las Vegas pro at the final table, Mike Matusow – nicknamed 'The Mouth' because he talks too much – was the first to be eliminated. 'Hey,' he said afterwards, 'money doesn't mean a thing to me. You all know that … I played the six best days of poker in my life, and when the TV comes out you'll see how great I played. I had a lot of confidence and a lot of chips.

'I knew I had a weak field. I was able do what I wanted when I wanted to. People started playing tight, which was really good for me. If you look at the chip position over the last few days, you'd see Mike Matusow's chips going up and up and up, but you never saw Mike Matusow in a pot. I was chop, chop, chopping away and never really risking any chips. That's what I wanted to do today [the final day]. I wanted to chop away to get about twelve million, and then get four- or five-handed, and then just rape them because these guys aren't short-handed players.'

The Hendon Mob

The Hendon Mob is an engaging collective of four British pros, who've expertly capitalised on the newfound popularity of poker in the UK, not least by having among their number TV actor Ross Boatman (who played Kevin Medhurst in the ratings-heavy ITV fireman drama *London's Burning*, and who starred in the West End run of *Dealer's Choice*). Other members include Ram 'Crazy Horse' Vaswani, Joe 'The Elegance' Beevers and Ross's brother Barney Boatman, who commentates on *Late Night Poker* and *Celebrity Poker Club*. Between them, they've won tournaments in France, Holland, Germany, Austria, Finland and Slovenia. Their website thehendonmob.com offers a superior database of champion players' winnings worldwide, alongside comprehensive global tournament listings and regular poker articles and columns – even the chance to become a 'Mobster of the Month'. The Mob play online under their own names at the Prima Poker network of virtual cardrooms (primapoker.com), often with tournament cash-bounties on their heads.

But somehow it didn't work out. Like people say, Mike talks too much.

The World Series of Poker began with the election by his peers of Johnny 'The Man' Moss in 1970. The following year Moss won it in competition, cementing his reputation as one of the greatest players who ever lived. The rest of the 1970s saw the title fall to each of the legendary poker names. Thomas 'Amarillo Slim' Preston, 'Puggy' Pearson, 'Sailor' Roberts and Doyle 'Texas Dolly' Brunson all won the world title before 1978 saw it go to Bobby Baldwin, now a Vegas casino boss, and 1979 to an unknown named Hal Fowler – who has never been heard of since.

The 1980s saw a procession of professional winners, from Stu 'The Kid' Ungar via Johnny Chan (twice) to Phil 'Poker Brat' Hellmuth, who have since become household names. (Well, in poker households.) With the exception of Ungar's remarkable comeback in 1997, the 1990s went on as they began, with a parade of pros famous – with honourable exceptions – for just fifteen minutes.

The head-to-head of the 1990 final table climaxed with another hand which has gone down in poker folklore, between a Vegas professional named Hans 'Tuna' Lund and a strong player from Britain, Iranian-born Mansour Matloubi.

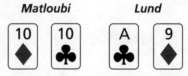

Matloubi   *Lund*

Pocket tens is a powerful hand, thought to be the sixth best of all hole-card combinations to be holding pre-flop. Accordingly, Matloubi bets. But Lund's ace with a decent kicker is also strong in heads-up play, so he calls.

For the moment, the tens have the edge. The flop comes:

Lund now has top pair. He's still losing the hand, but he doesn't know that, and wishes to sucker his opponent in. So he checks. Matloubi, sure that he's winning, goes all in. Lund calls, and the cards go on their backs. Lund grimaces as he see a pair of tens to his pair of nines. Then fourth street brings an ace.

The crowd goes wild as Lund pulls one of his five outs. Now Matloubi has only two – a third ten, out of forty-four unseen cards remaining in the deck, making him a 22–1 underdog. And the crowd goes even wilder as the board brings:

Yes, Matloubi's magic ten. His chip lead is now so huge that it does not take him long to finish off the disconsolate 'Tuna', and become the first and only Briton ever to win the world title (then worth $895,000).

Three other champs from the 1990s are still very much around: 1994's Russ Hamilton, 1995's Dan Harrington and 1998's Scotty Nguyen. Harrington has recently published a two-volume guide entitled *Harrington on Hold'em*, which is the book I would recommend after you've outgrown this one. Amid the countless other manuals, the best are Doyle Brunson's *Super System 2* and three volumes by 1993 champ Tom McEvoy and long-time top pro T. J. Cloutier: *Championship No-Limit and Pot-Limit Hold'em* (1997), *Championship Hold'em* (2002) and *Championship Tournament Practice Hands* (2003). The liveliest guide I know to the peculiar skills of online poker is Glenn McDonald's *Deal Me In!* (2005), with a foreword by the 2000 world champion, Chris 'Jesus' Ferguson.

You can buy whole books of odds, statistics and tables, if you must, but that way madness lies. These days, that kind of information is easily available on the web, at countless sites of varying quality. The only real way to learn how to play poker is to go out and do it, and keep doing it, until you find yourself growing more confident and more comfortable.

Then, one day, you may be able to add your name to this list:

World Series of Poker, $10,000 No-limit Hold'em Main Event Champions

1970	Johnny Moss (elected by vote)	–
1971	Johnny Moss	$30,000
1972	'Amarillo Slim' Preston	80,000
1973	Walter 'Puggy' Pearson	130,000
1974	Johnny Moss	160,000
1975	Brian 'Sailor' Roberts	210,000
1976	Doyle Brunson	220,000
1977	Doyle Brunson	340,000
1978	Bobby Baldwin	210,000
1979	Hal Fowler	270,000
1980	Stu 'The Kid' Ungar	385,000
1981	Stu 'The Kid' Ungar	375,000
1982	Jack Straus	520,000
1983	Tom McEvoy	580,000
1984	'Gentleman' Jack Keller	660,000
1985	Bill Smith	700,000
1986	Berry Johnston	570,000
1987	Johnny Chan	625,000
1988	Johnny Chan	700,000
1989	Phil Hellmuth Jr	755,000
1990	Mansour Matloubi	895,000
1991	Brad Daugherty	1,000,000
1992	Hamid Dastmalchi	1,000,000
1993	Jim Bechtel	1,000,000
1994	Russ Hamilton	1,000,000
1995	Dan Harrington	1,000,000
1996	Huck Seed	1,000,000
1997	Stu 'The Kid' Ungar	1,000,000
1998	Scotty Nguyen	1,000,000

1999	JJ 'Noel' Furlong	1,000,000
2000	Chris 'Jesus' Ferguson	1,500,000
2001	Carlos Mortensen	1,500,000
2002	Robert Varkonyi	2,000,000
2003	Chris Moneymaker	2,500,000
2004	Greg 'Fossilman' Raymer	5,000,000
2005	Joseph Hachem	7,500,000
2006	??????????	10,000,000(?)

See you at the final table...

Glossary

ACE-HIGH: a five-card hand containing an ace but no pair; beats a king-high, but loses to any pair or above

ACES UP: two pairs, one of which is aces

ACTION: the betting, as in 'The action's on you'

ADVERTISE: to reveal a bluff with the deliberate intention of being exposed as a 'loose' player

ALL IN: to bet all the chips you have left

ANTE: compulsory stake before the deal

ANTE UP: dealer's request for antes to be paid

AVATAR: online poker term for a player's computer-generated image

B&M: online term for a real card room, short for 'bricks and mortar'

BACK DOOR: term used when a straight or flush is filled on the turn and river cards

BACK TO BACK: two paired hole cards, as in 'aces back to back' or 'aces wired'

BAD BEAT: to lose a pot against the odds, a strong hand being beaten by a lucky one

BELLY HIT: to fill an inside straight

BET INTO: to bet before an apparently stronger hand, or a player who bet strongly on a previous round

BET THE POT: to bet the total value of the pot

BETTING INTERVAL: period during which each active player has the right to check, bet or raise; ends when the last bet or raise has been called by all players still in the hand

BICYCLE: the lowest possible straight, A-2-3-4-5

BIG BLIND: the largest ante; in Hold'em, usually compulsory to the player two to the dealer's left

BIG SLICK: A-K

BLIND (1): the compulsory bet or bets to the dealer's left

BLIND (2): to check or bet before receiving, or without looking at hole cards

BLOW BACK: to lose back most or all of one's profits

BOARD: the five communal cards revealed in the centre of a Hold'em game

BOAT: full house

BOBTAIL: *see* open-ended straight

BOSS: the strongest hand at that stage, as in 'boss trips'

BRING IT IN: to make the first bet

BUCK: the rotating button used by a professional dealer to indicate which player is notionally dealing the hand, and so should receive the last card

BULLET: an ace

BUMP: to raise (as in 'bump it up')

BURN: to deal off the top card, face down, before dealing out the cards (to prevent cheating); or to set aside a card which has been inadvertently revealed

BUST: a worthless hand, which has failed to improve as the player hoped

BUST A PLAYER: to deprive a player of all his chips; in tournament play, to eliminate a player

BUST OUT, BE BUSTED OUT: to be eliminated from a tournament by losing all your chips

BUSTED: broke, or tapped

BUSTED FLUSH: four-to-a-flush, which failed to fill up

BUTTON: see 'buck'

BUY-IN: the minimum amount of money required to sit down in a particular game or tournament

BY ME: an old-fashioned alternative to 'check' or 'fold'

CAGE: the casino's or card room's 'bank' where you exchange chips for cash or vice-versa

CALL: to match, rather than raise, the previous bet

CALLING-STATION: a player who invariably calls, and is therefore hard to bluff out

CARDS SPEAK: refers to a face-up declaration at the end of a hand, by which, even if a player has not realised he holds the winning hand, the dealer or other players can point this out on his behalf

CASE CARD: the last remaining card of a denomination or suit, when the rest have been seen, as in 'the case ace'

CASH IN: to leave a game and convert one's chips to cash, either with the dealer or at the cage

CATCH: to 'pull' the card or hand you want

CHASE: to stay in against an apparently stronger hand, usually in the hope of filling a straight or flush

CHECK: to offer no bet, reserving the right to call or raise if another player bets

CHECK-RAISE: *see* 'sandbag'

CINCH HAND: a hand that cannot be beaten; see also 'nuts'

COFFEE-HOUSING: to attempt to mislead opponents about your hand by means of devious speech or behaviour

COLD: a bad streak, as in, 'My cards have gone cold'

COLD DECK: a deck of cards 'fixed' in advance by a cheat

COME: to play an as yet worthless hand in the hope of improving it, as in playing 'on the come'

CONNECTORS: consecutive cards, such as 9-10 or J-Q which might make a straight

COWBOY: a king

CUT IT UP: to divide, or split, the pot after a tie

DEAD CARD: a card no longer legally playable

DEAD HAND: a hand no longer legally playable, owing to a dealing or playing irregularity

DEAD MONEY: *see* 'live one'

DEALER'S CHOICE: a game in which each dealer, in turn, chooses the type of poker to be played

DECLARATION: declaring by the use of coins or chips, in high-low poker, whether one is aiming to win the high or the low end of the pot, or both

DEUCE: a two, the lowest-ranking card in high poker

DOWN CARDS: hole (or pocket) cards

DRAWING OUT: to win a hand on the last card or cards, after staying with an inferior hand, 'on the come'

DRAWING DEAD: drawing to a hand that cannot win

DRIVER'S SEAT (in the): said of a player who is making all the betting and thus appears to hold the strongest hand

DROP: to fold

FAMILY POT: a pot in which most of the players are still 'in' before the flop

FIFTH STREET: the fifth and last communal card to be exposed in Hold'em, also known as the 'river'

FILL, FILL UP: to pull the card you are seeking

FISH: an inferior, losing player

FLAT-CALL: to call when a raise might have been expected

FLOORMAN: the card-room employee supervising a group

of tables, who is the ultimate arbiter of disputes

FLOP: the first three communal cards to be exposed in Hold'em

FLUSH: five cards of the same suit; ranks above a straight and below a full house

FOLD: to withdraw from, or give up, the hand

FOUR-FLUSH: four cards of the same suit, requiring a fifth to become a flush

FOUR OF A KIND: four cards of the same demonination; ranks above a full house and below a straight flush

FOURTH STREET: the fourth communal card to be exposed in Hold'em, also known as 'the turn'

FREE RIDE: to stay in a hand without being forced to bet

FREEROLL: online tournament with no entry fee but cash prizes

FREEZE-OUT: a game, usually a tournament, in which all players start with the same amount, and which continues until one player has won the lot

FULL HOUSE: a hand containing trips and a pair. Between two full houses, the higher trips win. Beats straights and flushes, loses to four of a kind

G-NOTE: a thousand-dollar bill

GRAVEYARD: the pre-dawn shift in a Las Vegas casino

GUTSHOT: the card needed to fill an inside straight

HEAD-TO-HEAD: *see* heads-up

HEADS-UP: a game between just two players, often the climax of a tournament

HIGH ROLLER: one who gambles for large amounts of money

HIGH-LOW: a species of poker in which the highest and the lowest hands share the pot

HIT: to fill, or obtain the card you are seeking

HOLE CARDS: in Hold'em, the two concealed cards dealt to each player at the start of a hand; see also 'pocket'

HOT: said of a player on a winning streak

HOUSE: full house, or 'boat'

IGNORANT END: the low end of a straight

IMPROVE: to pull a card or cards that better one's hand

IN: a player is 'in' (the hand) if he has called all bets

IN THE DARK: to check or bet blind, without looking at your cards

INSIDE STRAIGHT: four cards requiring (an unlikely) one in the middle to fill a straight, viz. 5-6-7-9; see also 'open-ended straight'

KIBITZER: a non-playing spectator, or railbird

KICKER: the subsidiary or 'side' card to a more powerful card or cards

KICK IT: to raise

KNAVE: a jack

KNOCK: *see* 'rap'

LAY DOWN: to reveal one's hand in a showdown; or to fold

LIMIT POKER: a game with fixed betting intervals, viz. £10–£20, £20–£40

LIMP IN: to call the big blind in late position

LITTLE BLIND: *see* 'small blind'

LIVE ONE: an inexperienced, bad or loose player; a sucker who apparently has money to lose

LOCK: a hand that cannot lose; see also 'cinch' and 'nuts'

LOOK: to call the final bet (before the showdown)

LOOSE: liberal play, usually in defiance of the odds

LOWBALL: a form of poker in which the lowest hand wins

MAKE (the deck): to shuffle

MARK: a sucker

MARKER: an IOU

MECHANIC: a cheat who manipulates the deck

MEET: to call

MOVE IN: to go all-in

MUCK: the discard pile, in which all cards are dead; also used as a verb

NUT FLUSH: the best available flush, i.e. an ace-high flush

NUTS: the best, unbeatable hand at any stage of a game

OFF SUIT: cards of different suits

ON TILT: playing badly, usually because of being stuck

ON YOUR BACKS: to turn your hole cards face up in a hand where there can be no more betting, i.e. after one or more players is/are all in

OPEN: to make the first bet

OPEN-ENDED STRAIGHT: four consecutive cards requiring one at either end to make a straight, viz. 5-6-7-8; also known as a two-way straight or a 'bobtail'

OUTS: the possibilities which would turn a losing hand into a winner

OVERCARDS: in Hold'em, cards higher than the flop cards, played in hope of catching a higher pair

OVER THE TOP: to re-raise

PAINT: any picture or court card

PAIR: two cards of the same denomination

PASS: to fold; occasionally (wrongly) used for 'check'

PICTURE CARD: king, queen or jack, also known as court or face cards

PIP: the suit symbols on a non-court card, indicating its rank

PLAY BACK (at): to re-raise

POCKET (in the): synonym for hole, as in 'pocket aces'

POCKET ROCKETS: a pair of aces in the hole

POSITION: your seat in relation to the dealer, and thus your place in the betting order, an important tactical consideration

POT: the chips at stake in the centre of the table

POT-LIMIT: a game in which the maximum bet is the total of the pot after a player has called

POT ODDS: calculating the percentage of the pot you are required to invest, as against your percentage chances of winning the hand, thus assessing the worth of the investment

PUT DOWN: to fold

RAGS: low, bad or unplayable cards

RAILBIRD: a non-playing spectator, or kibitzer, often used of a busted player

RAISE: to call and increase the previous bet

RAKE: chips taken from the pot by the dealer on behalf of the house

RAP: to knock the table, to indicate a check

READ: to try to figure out the cards your opponent is holding

RE-BUY: to start again, for an additional entry fee, in tournament play (where permitted)

REPRESENT: to bet in a way that suggests you are holding a particular (usually strong) hand

RE-RAISE: to raise a raise

RIFFLE: to shuffle chips

RING GAME: American term for cash games (as opposed to tournaments)

RIVER: in Hold'em, the fifth and final communal card to be exposed, also known as 'fifth street'

ROCK: an ultra-tight, conservative player

ROLL (a card): to turn a card face up

ROYAL FLUSH: A-K-Q-J-10 of the same suit. The best possible poker hand in all but wild-card games

RUN (1): synonym for a straight

RUN (2): a run of good cards, see also 'rush' and 'streak'

RUNNING BAD: on a losing streak

RUNNING GOOD: on a winning streak

RUSH: a run of good cards, see also 'run' and 'streak'. A player 'on a rush' may well 'play his rush', i.e. play an indifferent hand because he's feeling lucky and might win against the odds

SANDBAG: to check a strong hand with the intention of raising or re-raising

SATELLITE: a small-stakes tournament whose winner obtains cheap entry into a bigger tournament

SCHOOL: collective noun for the players in a regular game

SEE: to 'call'

SET: three of a kind or 'trips' (correctly used of a pair in the hand and one on the board)

SET YOU IN: to bet as much as your opponent has left in chips

SHILL: a card-room employee, often an off-duty dealer,

who plays with house money to start or fill up a game

SHOWDOWN: showing hole cards, after betting has ceased, to see which of the remaining players has won the pot

SIDE CARD: an unmatched card which may decide a pot between two hands otherwise of the same strength

SIDE POT: a separate pot contested by other players when one or more players are all-in

SLOWPLAY: to disguise the real value of a high hand by underbetting it, to tempt players with worse hands into the pot

SMALL BLIND: the smaller of the two antes; in Hold'em, compulsory to the player on the dealer's left

SOFTPLAY: to play gently against a friend

SPLIT (POT): a tie, or stand-off. Occasionally this can be agreed between two players before the hand is ended

SQUEEZE: to look slowly at the extremities of your hole cards, without removing them from the table

STACK: the pile of chips in front of a player, as in 'short stack'

STAND-OFF: a tie, in which the players divide the pot equally

STARTING HAND: the two hole cards in Hold'em

STAY: to remain in a hand with a call rather than a raise

STEAL: a bluff in late position, attempting to 'steal' the pot from a table of apparently weak hands

STEAMING: playing badly or wildly, going on tilt

STRADDLE: to make a voluntary blind raise before the deal

STRAIGHT: five consecutive cards, not of the same suit; beats trips, but loses to a flush and above

STRAIGHT FLUSH: five consecutive cards of the same suit. Beats everything but a higher straight flush, viz. a royal flush

STREAK: a run of good (or bad) cards, see also 'run' and 'rush'

STRING BET: an illegal bet in which a player puts some chips in the pot, then reaches back to his stack for more. He should declare a raise verbally before calling

STUCK: slang for losing

SUITED: cards of the same suit, as in 'A-Q suited'

SWEETEN (the pot): to raise

TABLE: can be used as a collective noun for all the players in a game, as well as for the green baize itself

TABLE STAKES: a poker game in which a player cannot bet more than the money he has on the table

TAP CITY: to go broke

TAP OUT: to bet all one's chips

TAPPED OUT: broke, busted

TELL: a giveaway mannerism or nervous habit which reveals the strength or otherwise of an opponent's hand

THREE-FLUSH: three cards of the same suit

THREE OF A KIND: three cards of the same denomination with two 'side' cards; beats two pairs, but loses to a straight or above. See also 'set' or 'trips'

TIGHT: a conservative player who plays only strong hands

TILT: see 'on tilt'

TOKE: a tip to the dealer (illegal in Britain)

TRAP: to check, or make merely a token bet, when holding a strong hand (with the aim of suckering another player into betting, then raising)

TREY: a three

TRIPS: three of a kind or a set. Beats two pairs but loses to a straight or above

TURN: the fourth communal card to be revealed at Hold'em, also known as 'fourth street'

TWO PAIRS: a hand containing two pairs plus a kicker; beats a pair but loses to trips or above

UNDER-RAISE: to raise less than the previous bet, allowed only if a player is going all-in

UNDER THE GUN: the player who is first to bet

UP CARD: an 'open' or exposed card

WHEEL: the lowest straight possible, A-2-3-4-5, also known as a 'bicycle'

WHIPSAW: to raise before, and after, a caller who gets caught in the middle

WILD CARD: a card designated as a joker, of any value

WIRED: said of two paired hole cards, as in 'aces wired' or 'aces back to back'